CALL ME VLADIMIR

A Personal Story
of the Rise of Russia
and the Fall of the Soviet Union

Dr. E. Scott Ryan

ISBN: 1-4196-8380-2
ISBN-13: 9781419683800

Published by Chosinness Productions:
Canada, Germany, Sri Lanka, Sweden and USA

Co-Sponsored by:
The International Institute for Forensic Education
The International Centre for Strategic Innovation
Forensic Counseling Associates
The Anti-Crime Sports and Education Alliance (which
receives profits from sales of this book)

Editor: Dawn Martin B.Sc. N., B.Ed.. Exec. Chair Retired
Teachers of Ontario, District Eight

Visit www.booksurge.com to order additional copies

CONTENTS

Appendix

Three Day Time Line of Events

August 19, 2001

7:00 am. Radio Rossii broadcasts the Declaration of the Soviet Leadership, in a hardline, conspiratorial, Communist "Moscoup" reversal of the glasnost and perestroika reforms of Mikhail Gorbachev.

8:00am. Russian People's Deputies are detained by the KGB and held on a military base.

9:10am. The quiet suburban Moscow residence of Tank Commander Vladimir Lubyanka and his wife, Raisa, is disturbed by a phone call from Dr. Ned Scott, an American professor, informing his long time friend, Vladimir, that the Moscoup has occurred.

10:15am. Vladimir meets with his dying mother who, with her last breath, asks for his promise to fulfill her prophetic vision of a free Mother Russia rising on the third day after her death, like Jesus, from the unfree tomb of Soviet Communism.

11:00am. Vladimir meets with his lover, Katherina, who informs him of her decision to go to the barricades at 12:30pm and stand with the freedom demonstrators at the Russian Parliament, referred to as the Russian White House, in supporting Boris Yeltsin.

12:30 pm. Vladimir returns to his home and informs his Communist wife that he is going to oppose the Moscoup despite her personal condemnation of his decision.

3:00 pm. Lieutenant Colonel Vladimir Lubyanka addresses his tank crews, in removing his name and rank designation, in presenting himself to them and others, not as a commanding officer, but as an unknown Russian patriot known only as Vladimir. He explains his decision and gives them the choice to freely decide to join him in taking his tank and going to the barricades to defend the freedom demonstrators.

5:15 pm. Vladimir arrives with his tank along with ten tank crews who follow him.

August 20, 2001

1:00am. News of the curfew declared by General Kalinin arrives at the barricades. This news is understood on both sides of the barricades as the sign that an attack is imminent.

1:15am. Vladimir decides to personally speak with each tank crew officer who followed him as to the dangers they face and the reasons for their decision to stay and fight.

2:30 pm. The decision is made to attack the White House with the code name, Operation Grom (Thunder), given to the military attack plan to be led by the Alpha Group.

5:45 pm. The Alpha Group led attack is planned for 2:00 am on Wednesday, Aug. 21.

August 21, 2001

2:00 am. The Alpha Group Commander, who in learning about an unknown tank commander named Vladimir and his stand at the barricades, refuses repeated direct orders to attack. Other commanders learn of this refusal to attack and they also refuse to attack. That commander was the 36th righteous man predicted in the Old Testament.

5:00 pm. Mikhail Gorbachev dismisses the Moscoup members from their state offices.

6:15 pm. Vladimir disappears into the celebrating crowds and disappears into history. He was last heard speaking about two fulfilled prophetic visions: the New Testament's three day Resurrection of Mother Russia from its Soviet tomb, and the Old Testament's 36th righteous man, who saved the world in saving those who took their stand for freedom.

CHAPTER ONE

Moscoupsiracy

The quiet suburban Moscow residence of Tank Commander Vladimir Lubyanka and his wife, Raisa, was abruptly disturbed by a 9:10 a.m. phone call on Monday, August 19, 1991.

He slammed down the phone jumping out of bed as she turned, still half asleep, towards her husband with the commanding countenance of a military commander's wife ordering him with her look to severely reprimand anyone so insubordinate as to interfere with her sleep.

"There's been a coup," he spoke as if he couldn't believe what he was saying.

"So another Moscoup with Mikhail shuffling ministers around trying to stay one step ahead of whomever threatens to step on his toes the hardest."

"God damn it Raisa, it's much more than that, they've got Gorbachev," he snapped, in a rising tone of voice expressing equal amounts of rage and impotency.

"How can that be?" she responded now fully awake and suddenly alarmed, sensing something new might touch the one thing she knew to be true, her life with her husband, "Gorbachev is on vacation in the Crimea and who are they?"

"Some kind of State of Emergency Committee of Ministers, Ned just phoned me, has illegally assumed control of the Government and they're holding Gorbachev under the pretext that he's tired and needs a rest."

The Lubyanka's friend, Dr. Ned Scott, an American professor who had maintained a close friendship with Vladimir ever since they were university roommates in the States 20 years ago, had called from the home of a Swedish journalist as soon as he heard the news.

"Ned wanted me to know first thing before I received any order."

"Isn't that considerate of him," Raisa replied with a bitter mocking sarcasm, "maybe Ned will bring a CNN crew over here with him for a Moscoup newscoup in interviewing you about your feelings concerning this coup."

"What's wrong, Raisa?"

"I'll tell you exactly what's wrong," she shot back with a glare of hysterical anger, "you're a senior tank commander in the most elite military unit in the Armed Forces, a Lieutenant Colonel of the Tamanskaya Guards Division, and now, yes right now, the KCB has a phone tap that you were contacted by an American just when Russian blood is likely to flow in the streets of Moscow."

"Vladimir, my dear Vladimir," her voice softened and the sarcasm dissipated, her fear overtaking her anger, as she reached out to him like a mother protecting her wayward son, "don't you see that no matter what happens, this committee or gang of hard liners is going to find political victims to purge, foreign conspirators to blame, and unreliable elements in the military to hold accountable for whatever goes wrong."

"We're in our middle forties, our daughter is getting her Ph.D. from Moscow State University, and we have a good life here no matter who runs the Soviet Union. You have a respected position in the military and even greater prospects in the future. Even if this current coup's leadership turns completely away from perestroika and glasnost, you're secure with the military - probably even more so than with new democratic forces like Yeltsin. In one year you can retire, and with your degrees in international relations you can work here or abroad as an analyst with the full support of the Soviet Union."

"My darling," as she spoke in an endearing whisper she embraced him with all her strength, "I want a live husband, a safe Soviet life, not a dead Russian hero."

He looked down as he sat on the bed next to her rather than at her as she continued to hold him close to her and pulled his head to her breasts.

"I loved you from the time we first met, and when I first saw you, I knew you would be my husband. Stay here with me and wait for orders. Do nothing until then and, then, do nothing other than what you're ordered to do - and that will be to keep order. No one, no Soviet apparatchik, no Russian democrat, no American, not even Ned Scott, will be able to blame you for just doing your duty."

"Raisa. I love you, too, but you're just wrong!" Vladimir spoke with the certitude of a new believer and with the severity of an executioner passing sentence upon himself.

"You're a history teacher; you teach Russian children about the Trials at Nuremberg where following orders was the best defense for the worst atrocities inflicted upon our country. That same mentality, that misleadingly sane rationality, that disastrously safe rationalization has been responsible for all kinds of horrendous crimes, including genocide, in so many corners of the world and even among ourselves."

"Leave it to the politicians, Vladimir, you're a military man, you're not a humanitarian, and your certainly not a liberal reformer."

"Maybe not," he replied, "but I'm still a human if not a humanitarian, and although I'm not a liberal, I do have a conscience, and while I'm not a reformer, I have to do something."

"Do what? Just what do you have to do? Just what? Tell me!"

"I don't know yet, but I do know that the answer to your question of just what... is...what's just.

Vladimir was telling the truth not only to his wife but, more importantly, to himself. It had taken him a long time, an entire life time, to arrive at this point in his life where he no longer felt that everything in life, that life itself, was just a product of chance.

In many ways Vladimir was a prototype of the official Russian, a moral schizophrenic, a believing atheist, a trained Marxist-Leninist in his mind but something else in his soul. The difficulty for Vladimir and millions like him was that he'd almost forgotten that he had a soul. Now, he remembered once again that, indeed, he did have a soul, albeit in deep Russian hibernation, a soul of his own separate from the state; but he still had no idea where to find it and time was running out.

It's so ironic, in some ways so tragic, isn't it, he thought to himself, that the most momentous decisions, ones that go beyond even one's own life and death, are ones that must be made on the spur of the moment, in response to an early morning telephone call.

He knew Raisa would never understand what he was going through, although she understood, perhaps better than he did everything else in life. If it weren't for Raisa, for her family's military connections, for her very practical, scientific even calculating way of making decisions, Vladimir Lubyanka, the son of Russian peasants would never have risen as far as he had. He owed her everything, but felt as if she held a lease not only on his body and mind, but on something more, his dormant soul. He was willing to lease his body and mind, but he resented the lease on his soul. His soul was in a deep Soviet hibernation and he longed for a Russian thaw with which to reawaken whatever was left of his soul.

He recalled an old Irish ballad about a man who spent the best years of his life in the arms of another man's wife...his mother. The Irish, he fondly mused in trying to escape the pressures of the moment by slipping into a Celtic trance, have the special talent of pleasantly shocking others with questions to which their ready answers provide an unexpected often tragic - comic relief.

While he dressed and frenetically threw together a hasty breakfast, he found himself in a self actuated trance, smiling to himself. Yes, he would disobey his wife's orders and he would not wait at home with her for military orders. He would go to his base but, first, on the way there he would visit that other women in the ballad, his mother, waiting in her nursing home for her son.

"I'm going to visit mother, she's expecting me," he spoke to his wife over his shoulder as he headed for the door.

"Good! maybe she'll talk some sense into her son's thick patriotic Russian bear brain," Raisa responded with self satisfaction, as if she were admonishing one of her delinquent high school students.

"Remember Vladimir," she raised her voice, as he stepped through the door, "your mother lost her husband in one war, she's much too ill to even think about the same thing happening to her son."

Leave it to Raisa, he thought, to have the last word. She always had the last word because he knew she was almost always right. However, this time, he knew that she would not have the last word for unlike most situations which she could accurately and even brilliantly analyze and predict, his decisions now would be made from the soul of his being. And Raisa, no matter how intelligent, could not predict the effects of what she didn't understand and didn't want to.

Vera Lubyanka, Vladimir's eighty year old mother, was the link to what he as a child once had, belief in the past and faith in the future. His father had died at home a few years after the end of World War II from his lingering war injuries. Vladimir, their only child, had been reared by his mother until he left for the junior military academy at the age of fourteen.

His mother represented the Russia of the Czars in contrast to his wife, a product of Marx and Lenin. Vera was a woman of faith and Raisa a believer in science. While his mother prayed to a God that created a material world for man, his wife worshipped man that created everything from a material world. In every way, physically, mentally, emotionally and spiritually, Vera was not only his mother but Mother Russia - and she was dying of terminal cancer.

The fact that Vladimir married a woman so unlike his mother gives the lie to Sigmund Fraudian's therapy, which in the name of this "odd studying the id psychology" tells us that we marry our mothers. Maybe there are a few odd incestuous neo-Fraudian ids out there who do marry their mothers, but Vladimir, at least, was not one of them.

He drove towards St. Basil's Cathedral to get a morning glimpse of its beautiful Byzantine towers, a practice he recently found himself doing more than he realized. Usually he would pick up a copy of Pravda, but there were none this morning and no other publications were anywhere to be seen. He stopped to walk over to the metro to find a newspaper and was stunned by the conspicuous absence of the omnipresent book and pamphlets sellers in the metro passages whose stark disappearance heightened the ambience of expectant eeriness.

5

The word was out over the radio, the word of the coup, and people were waiting at a loss for words as to what new words might replace the lexicon of perestroika and glasnost. Approximately fifty people stood across from the Council of Deputies - waiting and watching - their number slowly beginning to grow.

As he drove north in his new Lada he noticed four armored personnel carriers driving around the square. He knew that Moscow had a higher concentration of troops at this time of year to help with the harvest; but he also knew that the APCs were not there, this day, to help with the potato crop.

[Handwritten margin notes:]

APC

YEARS
1985
TILL
1991

PERESTROIKA
RESTRUCTING SOVIET ECONOMY &
(REFORM) BUREAUCRACY
BY MIKHAIL GORBACHEV

GLASNOST A POLICY OF OPENNESS
& FREEDOM OF INFORMATION
BY M G

CHAPTER TWO

APCs Armored Personnel Carriers and the Armor of a Person's Conscience

Vladimir pushed the accelerator to the floor hoping to quickly pass by these armored personnel carriers. He sped by them in leaving them behind in the dust of his side view mirror in fixating his gaze further ahead than he could see. As a career military officer, these military vehicles were more familiar to him than his own car. Nevertheless, he was afraid to look back into the mirror lest the A.P.C.s mirror the dust in his soul raised by a very different A.P.C... the Armor of a Person's Conscience.

He kept the pedal to the metal, an Americanism he remembered from his university days of high speed driving in the States with Ned. At that time they were graduate student roommates at the Rockefeller College in Albany, New York, and it was fun to speed on the New York State Thruway. It was fun to save time in getting to one's destination and it always gave him a high. Now, however, there was no high or low road to take in the no road of not knowing what he was rushing to in knowing what not to do, but not what to do.

He knew only one thing for certain, that this was not the time to wait for orders. For the first time in his life, for the very first time since he left home and enrolled in the junior military academy some thirty years before, he knew that he had to create his own orders for himself, to make a personal command decision on matters of life and death which would call for the same decision from and for others.

Those others were not only his loyal tankers, the men of the Tamanskaya Guards who named the T-72 tanks that were used to awe visitors, military and civilian alike, with their world renown demonstrations of the T-72's power and maneuverability, but his wife Raisa, his friend, Ned, and most of all his lover, Katharina... all of whom would live or die in one way or another by what he would decide to do in the next few hours. For their sake, more than his own, he had to know more than what was simply right, he had to

7

know something far more complex - the right answer to the right question for himself, for them, for everyone.

For three decades he'd been trained that any order no matter how bad was better than no order, and that a bad order that was clear was better than a good order that was unclear. Complexity was bad and simplicity was good in a "Keep it simple, stupid, subculture of simplistic stupidity." He believed it and he lived it and he didn't know what else to believe. He suspected, however, that he had believed a lie and he promised himself that he would no longer live nor die for a lie.

The essential personality ingredient a professional soldier cannot live without, he smiled to himself, was a sense of humor, especially in the face of death. Civilians accustomed to a safe life have the comfort of being sentimental and the luxury of being morose about death; but a soldier, a real soldier, can only live by laughing in the face of death. Belatedly, he glanced in the rear view mirror to find himself well beyond sight of the APC's as he started to laugh, laughing hysterically at himself. Imagine, he thought, here I am rushing to I don't know what. He thought about the thoughtlessness of the ingrained military reflex, the hurry up and wait, always hurrying and then waiting according to some orders from higher-ups who in turn were rushing and waiting for their orders.

Without the shadow of any doubt, he could assert from his three decades in the military, the more complex the situation the more simple the order. The highest higher-up, the all knowing source of ultimate authority, without fail, would issue orders with the knowledge of a know nothing causing everyone below to fail - the unlucky ones with their lives. This chain of command put commanders in chains and both former superpowers, the USA in Vietnam and the U.S.S.R. in Afghanistan, lost to enemies who fought without chains. The Gulf War in no way disproved his axiom, rather, it confirmed it by proving that smart bombs are smarter than the smartest military mind.

Still driving at breakneck space and listening to the car radio reports of the military being deployed to maintain law and order, he asked himself the one question that would guarantee his automatic excommunication from the universal military brotherhood: "Whose Law and What Order?" Lieutenant Colonel Vladimir Lubyanka could hear and see all of military history synthesized in one operational commandment: Thou Shalt Not Think for Oneself. The greatest danger to the military machine, the most egregious affront to the military mind and the unforgivable sacrilege against its belief system was not treason, but reason. The treasonous act of giving information to the enemy might interfere with one victory, but it would not guarantee final defeat. Giving information to oneself and acting upon it without orders, however, was the one act that would lead to defeat for it took final victory from the military and gave it to the individual. Vladimir decided to think for himself, thereby militarily excommunicating himself.

His decision was not based on a newly found pacifism nor had he decided to become a conscientious objector. To the contrary, Vladimir had decided that he would fight, but it would be his fight, not others. He would fight for others, yes, but not by the order of others. Above all else, in heaven and hell and in between, it was his fight and he would fight with everything he knew about the military for what he knew next to nothing about, himself. He smiled as the good soldier he was in facing death, smiling that after 30 years he would take a personal stand, make a free choice, issue a life and death military order not as Lt. Col. Vladimir Lubyanka, the representative of the establishment, an officer of the elite Tamanskaya Guards, but as Vladimir, as a man, as finally a free man.

What did he know, specifically, right now, right this minute, he asked himself. He answered that he knew that what he knew best was how to command and deploy T-72 tanks, the pride of the Soviet Army and his personal joy. He also knew as he saw the outline of his mother's nursing home in the distance come into sight that he'd finally freed himself of that reflexive military fear of complexity. Most of all, he'd found the right answer to the right question, that he was a free man, first, and a military man, second.

Like a dying man whose life passes before him just before he enters into the next life, his life was flashing in front of him as he prepared himself, as the doctors told him, to see his dying mother for the last time. What an irony about life and death, he reflected, that living and dying seem to be so positively correlated. His mother seemed more alive to him now that she was dying, and he felt more alive now that he faced the likely prospect of his own death.

CHAPTER THREE

Motherly Icon of Mother Russia

He started to pump the car brake pedal, in relishing his calculated luck in not being stopped by the police, whose attentions were preoccupied by the ambience of incipient anarchy as he broke every driving law in speeding across Moscow. Approaching the nursing home and his awaiting mother, waiting for him so she could die, he felt a premonition deep in himself - beyond his mind or emotions - that his dying mother knew more and expected more of him than he could envision. This invisible fact of life, vision obscure in its origin but clear in its effect, was the greatest difference among so many between his wife and his mother. Whereas Raisa knew everything, his mother saw everything. While his wife knew so many things that his mother didn't, Raisa knew only what was certain. His mother, to the contrary, was certain only of what she could envision, and what she could see in her visions she was certain nothing could prevent. The vision of his mother was the icon of Mother Russia, and like her she was old and near dead, but still alive.

Coming to a stop, he released his seat belt sensing the futility and the irony in the present situation of any safety precaution. As he stepped out of his car, away from the confined safety to he knew not what awaited him from his mother, Vera, his wife, Raisa, his American friend, Ned, his lover, Katharina, his country, be it Soviet or Russian, or himself, as an elite officer and a common man, he realized - suddenly and completely - that while freedom can lead to safety, safety can never lead to freedom.

He stood on the sidewalk in front of the nursing home for a few moments in slowly breathing in and out, in creating slow and deep breaths until he caught his breath and felt ready to be with his mother for the last time. Despite the scarcity of goods and services in Moscow's nursing homes, his mother was well looked after in receiving all kinds of little presents and daily visits from the elderly parishioners of nearby St. Nicholas Russia Orthodox Church. Vera Lubyanka was not only an old time believer, but, according to the Party, a religious fanatic with Czarist delusions. She had never suffered for her religious beliefs, as had so many others of her generation, due to the fact that her deceased husband was a highly decorated war hero. She was further protected by the fact that her son had been removed from her bourgeois Russian Orthodox Church as the Party derisively described it, young enough to be reeducated in Marxist-Leninist Orthodoxy at the Soviet Union's premier military academies, or so they thought.

Vladimir as a young boy and later as a young man, had done very well in his schooling, and most importantly for his career, his Marxist schooling. He attained straight As in every course on dialectical materialism, historical inevitability, economic determinism, Hegelian philosophy, proletarian dictatorship and class conflict. He knew how to diagnose capitalist injustices and conceptually reconstruct how the social ideological superstructure obscured the material base of all reality and manipulated the masses by means of the opiates of (1) religion and bourgeois morality according to the very best Marxist analysis in reference to every conceivable human and social problem. Nevertheless, he never forgot his mother's simple teachings that made him doubt if Marxism ever knew what was right even if it did know what was wrong. In re-visualizing his mother's visions, he could see more clearly than ever before that the Communists were totally blind as to what was plainly inside and in the sight of every person - freedom.

(1) KARL MARX said Religion was the opium of the people

CHAPTER FOUR

Flashbacks

As he walked into the lobby of the nursing home to sign in at the visitor's desk, his mind flashed back two decades to the time he signed in at Brubacher Hall as Ned Scott's roommate at Rockefeller College. How shocked he was to discover that his American roommate had a picture, just like his Russian mother had, of Jesus on his desk. He was further surprised to discover that his university roommate actually believed in a Christian God. They further surprised each other in finding that not only could they talk to each other about anything, but that they liked to talk to each other about anything.

Walking heavily and hesitantly up the long narrow and rickety flights of stairs to his mother's room in the top floor, he recalled being called into the President's Office at 2:00 p.m. on September 1, 1771, immediately upon his arrival in Albany, New York, as an exchange graduate student in international relations. After so many years and after so many changes in relations between nations and, more significantly, in his relationship with himself, Vladimir could recall even more visibly than before every detail of that meeting with President Vincent Sullivan.

He remembered being lost for close to an hour trying to find which of the three identical twenty five story towers of the University at Albany housed the President's office. The architecture of the Mega University of The State University of New York at Albany had been designed by some renowned international architect for a new university in Saudi Arabia, with its sweeping white colors being amply suited to the sand dunes of the desert. Somehow, Allah knows, this university of the desert wound up in snow bound Albany, New York, according to the political designs of one Governor Nelson A. Rockefeller. Nelson A. was the Exhibit A of the American golden calf and the political epitome of the ruling Sheik of New York State in terms of both public and private power and influence.

However, unlike the European robber baron families who robbed enough to attain a title of nobility, the Rockefellers took their noblisse oblige seriously and through the political career of Nelson

A. Rockefeller they proved that, at least in their case, there could be conspicuous exceptions to the paristocitic noability of inherited wealth. During his governorship, Nelson A. Rockefeller created a benevolent despotism in his Grade A New York State University system. Whatever Nelson wanted, Nelson got. And, fortunately, he wanted superior programs and excellent universities since high grade public projects were more likely to help him make the grade as a future President of the United States.

Nelson turned out to be a good democratic despite being a Republican, in terms of being a man for the people, if not of the people. In wanting him to be recognized as such, the Rockefellers got a coffee commercial to remove the lyrics "rich as Rockefeller" so that Nelson, thereafter known as Rocky - not to be confused with Sylvester "Rocky I, II, III, etc." Stallone- would be somewhat analogously perceived as a fighter for the people. In a most unusual anomaly for the superrich, Rocky did win some heavyweight bouts for the people by expanding educational financial assistance through the New York State Regents Scholarship program, and by introducing highly sophisticated and specialized professional education programs with the State University at Albany as his readily available standard bearer.

It's been hypothesized that power corrupts and absolute power corrupts absolutely. However, Nelson, alias Rocky, proved in his New York State experiment as Governor that benevolent power can be absolutely benevolent as well as powerful. He showed that as long as the source of power and the recipients are on the same wavelength, the right thing can happen for both right and wrong reasons. Whereas other politicians have been investigated for being "on the take" in order to get rich quick, Nelson was "on the give" in order to quickly get what he wanted from the poor in making them less poor.

Luckily for Vladimir Lubyanka, for his American roommate, Ned Scott, and for President Vincent Sullivan, they were all on the same wavelength, the receiving wavelength from Governor Rockefeller, or Nelson A, as his friends called him, or Rocky, as the people called him. If they hadn't been on the same wavelength, they would not have been there. In retrospect, Rocky was the best professor the international students and professors ever had for he taught them a cardinal lesson about America that money talks and if you get in its way, you'll walk, or be walked away.

"Come in Mr. Lubyanka, or shall I address your as First Lieutenant," President Sullivan good naturedly greeted rather than questioned him, as he entered an office three times the size of any room he'd seen in the Soviet Union outside of the former Czarist residence. He took his seat, the one seat the secretary had escorted him to directly across from and facing the President's high light oak desk. The office appeared to him to be more of a sprawling information command center, which it was, than a room. He awkwardly took his seat and then, just as awkwardly, quickly stood up again as Sullivan arose and walked around his desk - taking the better part of a minute - with the assistance of a cane to heartily and heartedly shake Vladimir's hands. As they shook hands he tried not to notice the braces on the President's foot and lower leg, the remnant, he was later to learn, of childhood polio.

"Well, what shall it be, Mr. or Lieutenant?" Sullivan again pointedly but still good naturedly inquired, as Vladimir felt more comfortable with President Sullivan and, strangely, less comfortable with himself.

"I'd prefer that you just call me Vladimir, sir."

"Then, young man, if that's your preference, rest assured or as one might be accustomed to in military parlance," President Sullivan continued his sentence by assuming and the posture of a drill instructor, "parade rest, as you were, at ease… all of us at this university shall just call you Vladimir!"

"Yes, sir!" he responded as if acknowledging an order.

"Vladimir, we'll establish a special understanding between the two of us as of this moment, I won't address you as Lieutenant if you don't address me as Sir."

"Yes Sir," he blurred out nervously, "I mean, excuse me, most certainly, President Sullivan", Vladimir responded in trying to regain his self composure by verbalizing what he could master of the King's English accent from his summer courses at Oxford.

"Call me Dr. Sullivan, that's more common around here," he responded in a clearly clear non-Oxford, mid-western American accent, while continuing to look at him in a direct even piercing way that Vladimir was not accustomed to.

"This morning I interviewed another new graduate student, an American by the name of Ned Scott, who made the same mistake of addressing me as sir. Sir is a military term as well as a British remnant of a class position, a title of sorts, and since I'm neither your commanding officer, titled, nor British, none of which I've ever aspired to, let's forever henceforth abandon siring, which is academically equivalent to sinning, at this university."

Not knowing what to say or quite what Dr. Sullivan was all about, and feeling increasingly uneasy, ironically more with himself than with him, Vladimir again reflexively responded with a Yes ... catching himself a split second before falling back into that ingrained habit and academic mortal sin of siring.

"Now, Vladimir, while this is as you are indubitably aware an education not a military institution, decisions is made in both the USSR and USA in an often less than democratic fashion. There are some academic types who, you will undoubtedly hear from later, accuse me of being the worse thing possible in the university world, an authoritarian."

"I'm used to that, Dr. Sullivan."

"Well put, Vladimir, I'm sure you are; but I don't agree with that label, at least in reference to myself for exercising legitimate authority in the cause of a higher purpose, a good purpose and a necessary purpose, which is not synonymous with authoritarianism."

"My function," Sullivan continued, "is to fulfill my mandate to the Council of Trustees of the Rockefeller Graduate School, to exercise my authority in the way I see fit in order to fit different people together so that in the future all people can live together in a different way, hopefully, in a peaceful way."

"Accordingly, I've made a decision about you and Ned Scott, that the two of you will be roommates at this university. I haven't yet relayed my decision, which I intend to do after talking to you, and which decision will be very clearly and unmistakably indicated as being my decision rather than yours or Ned's, so that there will be no misunderstanding or difficulty with any Soviet or American military authorities.

"Dr. Sullivan, if I may inquire what do the American military authorities have to do with this decision of yours?"

"Very frankly, Vladimir, your roommate Ned Scott is ,like yourself, a First Lieutenant with the slight difference of being in a different army," Sullivan spoke slowly and carefully, emphasizing the word slight, in watching and waiting as if anticipating a reaction that he expected and had already dismissed.

Now he understood what President Sullivan, or as he preferred to be called, Dr. Sullivan, was all about, and his displeasure showed through despite his best but fumbling attempt to hide it.

"You're less than pleased, I can see, and I understand more than you may think why you're upset about my decision. However, with all due candor, I must tell you face to face that this is my decision, my final decision, and I'm not going to change it regardless of your feelings and regardless of Ned Scott's similar feelings."

"Dr. Sullivan," Vladimir spoke in finding his courage to respond, "I am a newcomer and a visitor not only at this school but in this country, and, if I may also speak with all due candor, I see no reason why two individuals, total strangers to each other, should be forced to room together when it's a highly distasteful proposition for both of them."

"Vladimir, I could respond with the military refrain that yours is not to reason why but to do or die, or I could use your own description of yourself as a newcomer to define it as coming to whatever's new," Sullivan answered him with an engaging and contagious good nature that Vladimir realized had the effect of disarming any and all opposition - as it was disarming his own.

This man with a cane was truly a great man in compensating for his crippled body by making others compensate for their crippled minds. Because of him, Vladimir and Ned developed a lifelong friendship with a different view of not only each other and others, but of themselves. Vince Sullivan, without equal, was the most skillful chief executive officer - in getting people not only to do what he wanted but to want to do what he wanted - in any institution, public or private, academic or corporate, in the country. Vladimir had never met anyone anywhere nearly as talented in administration - in ministering to others to want what he wanted - in any government, company or church in the world. He instinctively felt, and correctly so, that no matter how me might protest, Sullivan would not only have his way; but the more he talked, the more he would find himself not only accepting what he said but agreeing with it, culminating in the inevitable of being personally convinced by Vince.

"I've reviewed both yours and Ned Scott's records and personal files, and believe me, my decision is one that's best for both of you. Your father died as a result of injuries received in fighting the Nazis - so did Ned's father. You've attained full scholarship assistance from your government and from this university; and Ned, also, has been granted full scholarship assistance from us and from his government. You're a First Lieutenant in Armor and he's a First Lieutenant in Field Artillery, both combat arms branches. You were educated according to the secular dogma of Marxist-Leninism and he's been educated according to Catholic dogma by Jesuits. You're both products of extremely rigorous, dissimilarly similar educational systems for the propagation of secular and spiritual salvation, respectively, by means of truly exclusive faiths with a less than respectful history of tolerance for the truths of others."

"God knows" Sullivan spoke, and then corrected himself, "or maybe Marx knows," he added as a courtesy to Vladimir as he continued to speak, while leaning over his desk projecting himself towards him as if his life depended on convincing him, "what will happen to these two faiths." As he listened, Vladimir felt something in himself becoming more and more convinced by Vince Sullivan, "but I'm responsible for what will happen to you two young men."

"You and Ned Scott are not only graduate students and professional soldiers, you're much more than that, both of you are representatives of a new breed, you're the combat intelligentsia, educated and trained for ideological as well as military warfare. Because of your backgrounds whether you stay in the military or not, the time will come when you will not only follow orders, but give orders. Your decisions, then, will go far beyond how to take and hold a military position. In the future, what you decide will determine whether we have more justice or more oppression, more freedom or more slavery, more war or more peace, more life or more death. Furthermore, Vladimir, everything I've just mentioned could depend on just one man's decision, on just one order, the order he gives to himself, the final order not only for himself but, very possibly, for the world.

He leaned back as far as his red leather recliner chair would go and gazed at the ceiling for a full minute as if waiting for a confirmation from above. Vladimir felt like stepping forward and proclaiming his conversion to the new gospel of one's own order espoused by this most impressive and inspiring man, but he hesitated in order to think, to find the words best suitable to match his feelings.

(2) COMBAT ARMS US ARMY 3
INFANTRY
ARTILLERY
ARMOR

CHAPTER FIVE

Canvinced by Vince

While searching for the words he thought of a new word, since he was more than convinced by Vince he felt that another word, a further word, was needed to express his feeling, his new belief.

"I can," he responded without the need for any more thinking.

"I'm CANVINCED!" he almost shouted taking advantage of his lack of familiarity with proper English to create a new word, proper or not."

"I'm *canvinced,* Dr. Sullivan, if I may be so improper with the King's English, because not only do I agree with and believe in what you've said, but more than that, I know it can be done, therefore, I feel and I am *canvinced.*"

"My dear young man," Sullivan replied with equal countenances of awe and admiration, "as a Doctor of English Literature, I must inform you that, indeed, your new word is improper. Yes, Vladimir, it's a quite improper, in fact, it's more than improper for it goes beyond what's proper to what's more than proper, to a new truth. Your addition to our language is gloriously improper, a tribute to me in one small respect but a tribute to you in every respect."

He recalled how Sullivan personally walked with him, at a half gait with the assistance of his cane, from his office to the shuttle bus stop which would take him to Brubacher Hall located approximately three miles south of the main campus on State Street in downtown Albany. Walking with a short leg shuffle along side him to the bus, a most unusual gesture for a very busy university president not to mention one burdened with the need of a cane, Sullivan said nothing, a strange reaction from a man so fluent and proficient in *canvincement.*

As he stepped forward to get on the bus, he turned to say goodbye to President Sullivan, and to thank him for personally escorting him to the shuttle. Before he could say anything, Sullivan put his hand on his shoulder and with a watery haze in his eyes half way between tears and joy as if overcome by fate and faith and stated, "Vladimir, for the first time at this university my own words are as real for me as I've tried to make them real for others. I verbalize these words every day hoping to convince myself in convincing others. Now, for the first time, I'm convinced. Don't thank me, I should thank you - thank you, Vladimir, thank you very much!"

CHAPTER SIX

Vera Lubyanka's Last Day and Lasting Vision of an Entombed Mother Russia of Freedom Rising on the Third Day

"Your mother is ready to see you," the hospice nurse spoke, as she came out the door of his mother's room and walked quietly down the stairs, announcing without words that this would be Vera Lubyanka's last visitor, today, and that today was her last day.

Entering her room reminded him in a stark and strange analogy of first entering Vince Sullivan's office, nervously not knowing what to expect or to say. Yet there was a very logical reason for his mind flashing back to visually and verbally recall every detail of his meeting with Sullivan for he was like his mother, a visionary. They were both prophetic visionaries who saw beyond the limits of their respective realities. The respective difference between them was that Vince's prophetic yet logical secular visions were contingent on what could be, what might be; whereas his mother's religious visions were not limited to the realities of this world but, rather, they saw reality in a mysterious way beyond logic through personal revelation as to what would be, and what must be.

He approached her hesitantly and anxiously, fearfully stepping closer as if stepping to the side of death, holding back his tears when she embraced him with what little strength remained in her dying body. He sat down on the bed close to her side so their bodies were touching and looked into her light blue eyes which both startled and assured him with their shining clarity and their projection of mischievous joyfulness.

Despite all his years of military training and his degrees in international relations, he knew that at the deepest level of living and of dying, his mother knew something he didn't. Suddenly, he felt like a four year old going to his mother for a pre-kindergarten lesson about something in life he'd just encountered and needed his mother to explain to him.

"My son," she started to speak in short gasps of breath as she sat propped up in her bed with high white pillows accentuating her still long and soft brown hair only slightly streaked with gray, "don't worry about me, I know why I'm here and where, very soon, I'll be. It's you that I'm worried about."

"I'm fine mother. Please, at a time like this I don't want you to worry yourself with any concern about me," he replied, in meaning yet doubting what he was saying, for he was not fine. He wanted to see what his mother could see that allowed her, better than any professional soldier he'd ever seen, to smile so - in the face of death.

"I'm smiling my dearest darling son because now is the time for you to fulfill my vision," she spoke with the appearance of senility but the substance of insight.

"When your father died when you were just a little one, I received a vision that you were born to me for a special mission, of a mission of rising, a mission of finding a new life over an old death," Vera Lubyanka whispered, as she started to fade from her own life.

Realizing that she had at best only seconds left, he put his ear next to her lips to show her that he would not only hear her last words but fulfill her vision and complete his mission.

"Russia died in 1917 but Mother Mary came to me with a vision that Mother Russia would rise once again, and that my son would be the one who would take the first step to show the way. In the vision, Russia, like Jesus, goes into a tomb for three days and then rises again. The door of the tomb is opened by you, Vladimir, so that not only Russia but the world will have a chance, a new chance, but more than a new chance at life it will be the chance at a new life. The last part of the vision, my darling Vladimir, is that I will die on the first day, and on the third day the vision will have been accomplished."

"I'm ready to die now if you can live for my vision and for your mission," she could barely whisper as her breathing began to fade.

"Yes, mother, yes, I can, I can, I can, I can," he continued to whisper in her ear as her breathing finally ended with his assurances. She died with that mischievous smile, with which he was so astonished but no longer surprised to observe, that radiated more victory over death than any heroic battlefield courage in the face of death.

He sat there motionless for what seemed to be an eternity in the presence of eternity. He recalled the prophetic hope in President Sullivan's eyes, as he continued to contemplate the assurance of hope, the vision of faith in his mother's radiant smile. He reflected how being *convinced* by the secular hope of Vince Sullivan was one and the same as the "I can" in response her vision of faith. The difference between the secular vision of Sullivan and the religious vision of his mother was less a difference in kind than a difference in degree. His mother was just one step ahead and, now, one place beyond.

He finally stood up and finally understood the parable of Jesus that one must die to oneself in order to live; the opposite of which is evil: simply live spelled backwards. How true it is he marveled with the new realization of an old proverb that the most complex truth can be explained by the simplest paradox. He'd promised to fulfill his mother's deathbed vision not as a death wish, but as a wish for facing death as a way of seeing life. I can, I can, I can he repeated to himself, and because of her vision he was certain that he could and he would face his own death in order to see what she had been able to see. Yes, he learned the most important lesson in life - the lesson of life and death - from his dying mother's living vision, and no matter what, he would not envision anything less.

Vladimir reported his mother's demise to the nurse at the front desk with a resigned calm and a calm resignation that she was clearly unaccustomed to, in her wondering whether Mrs.Lubyanka's son forgot how to care or just cared to forget, whether he no longer cared or could no longer show that he cared. He turned to leave and stopped, finding himself face to face with his old friend, Ned Scott. His personal confirmation of no matter what was confronted with Ned's person, confirming one thing: Ned knew what the matter was and he'd come after him at the risk of his own life to tell him.

"I'm very sorry about your mother, Vladimir. I called Raisa and she told me you were here. She didn't want to tell me where you were, but I insisted we must talk now!"

CHAPTER SEVEN

Ned Scott, Peacebroker, in Brokering the Need with the Demand for Freedom

His old friend, Ned Scott, who'd become a professor of criminology and conflict resolution at an American University, had a unique personal ability and an innate skill supplemented by professional training of obtaining information that very few people knew and discovering facts that even fewer people wanted to know. After rooming with Vladimir for a year at the University at Albany, he was called to serve out his military commitment with the United States Army in Vietnam. After experiencing that strategic and moral debacle, he left the army and served himself by earning a Ph.D. as the educational passport and academic meal ticket to a university professorship.

Having spent the first half of his life being educated by the church and the military, he spent the second half as a professor educating himself and doing penance for his military sins by developing a specialization as a professional peacebroker, defined as a professional who finds the right information about peace in brokering the need with the demand for peace. As his penance, he'd made a vow of obedience to himself to serve peace with a dedication that surpassed the blind obedience required in the military, and he replaced it with the blinds of moral obedience to block out any obstacle to peace.

If he ever had to fight in whatever way again, he would fight for peace. Vladimir, ever since he'd been *canvinced* by Vince Sullivan that the ideology of the person rather than of the people is the way to peace, felt the same. In addition, he experienced almost the identical reaction to his country's war in Afghanistan that Ned had to his in Vietnam. The difference between them was that Vladimir waited longer until making the same decision about himself, waiting until he could no longer wait any longer, waiting until now.

For almost two decades they'd been in touch; in fact, it was at an international peace conference in Visby, on the Swedish island of Gotland in the Baltic Sea that through Ned, he met Katharina, his lover, a half-Russian, half ethnic German distant relative of Catherine the Great, the German Empress of Russia. Ned had always impressed him with what seemed to be a moral fixation on right and wrong; yet this morality was never fixed and seemed to be even more relative than that of Marxism, which justified any immoral means in the cause of its own morality. You always knew what was absolutely right in Marxism, he reflected, even when you knew that you were required to do what was absolutely wrong. Marxism, he knew from experience, by fixating morality on itself, by initiating any immoral means to its moral end, ended as it began in amorality.

Ned's morality, which he'd slowly come over two decades not only to understand and accept but to embrace, was that the absolute was ever present but never fixed. He recalled Ned's Jesuitical response in one of their late night discussions as students that the proposition that there is no absolute is, in itself, an absolute proposition. Yes, there was an absolute right and an absolute wrong. He knew what he believed and he believed what he knew, but he didn't know where to find it. His mother had seen it, but before he could see it he would have to find it for himself.

Ned, who had been so instrumental in introducing him to a new way of thinking about truth so long ago, was at this moment once again with him for the new and final moment of truth: a moment in life and a moment beyond life for a final moment of truth about life.

How ironic, he commented to himself, that one finds oneself at the wrong place and the wrong time in trying to find out what's right. At this very moment he found them to be at both the wrong place at the right time, and the right place at the wrong time. It was the wrong place for Ned to be at the right time for Vladimir; and it was the right place for Ned to be at the wrong time for Vladimir. It was the wrong place for Ned because he was an American, an all too easily labeled agent provocateur for any wrong doing; and it was the right time for Vladimir, a seasoned tank commander in a season of civil unrest and a time of military danger. It was the right place for Ned because he knew as usual, what others didn't know; and it was the wrong time for Vladimir because he knew that his time had run out.

"Let's go into this side room," Ned gestured for Vladimir to follow him, as he led the way and entered the room, immediately turning to check and secure the lock on the door.

"Have you heard anything?" he asked Vladimir.

"Only some reports over the radio that forces are being called in to maintain order."

"Before you report to your base, I want you to know what's happening, and I want you to meet with me a little later when I get more information," Ned spoke without waiting for Vladimir to do more than nod assent with his eyes.

"At one this morning, the Tass Director was called to the Central Committee of the Communist Party for a meeting with officials to prepare him for officially approved reporting on this morning's coup. Gorbachev had been warned before by Shevardnadze and more recently by Yakolev, who even named names, that this would happen. He foolishly dismissed these warnings, foolishly is more than an understatement for his incredible passivity, in stating that 'they lack the courage to stage a coup'!"

"As late as 4:00 P.M. yesterday, Gorbachev was working in his vacation dacha at Foros in the Crimea on the union treaty speech he was to sign on Tuesday with the presidents of the Russian and Kazakh republics. He telephoned his aide, Georgi Shakhnazarov, who was vacationing nearby without giving the slightest indication that anything was amiss. Then, at 10 minutes to 5:00, the chief of security entered Gorbachev's office and told him that a group of people wanted to see him. When Gorbachev tried to phone Moscow, he found that his phone lines and communications had been cut."

"This visiting delegation of sorts was composed of Yuri Plekhanov, Chief of State Security, Valeri Boldin, Gorbachev's own Chief of Staff, Oleg Baklanov, Deputy Chairman of the National Defense Council, Oleg Shenin, a Party apparatchik, and General Valentin Varennikov. The State Committee for the State of Emergency, a suitably contrived name for such a misstated statement of a state coup mistake, put the demand to Gorbachev that he sign a decree to proclaim an emergency and to turn all his authority over to Vice President Gennadi Yanayev."

"What did he do?"

"For once in his diplomatic life he was wonderfully undiplomatic in telling them all to go to hell."

"Good for him!" Vladimir replied.

"Yes, and good for all of us, because if he had gone along and done what they demanded, we'd all be goners."

"Nevertheless, I don't know how long he can hold out. I've learned that KGB troops have his house surrounded, and they've driven tractors across the runway of the Cape Foros airport to keep his TU-134 presidential jet from taking off."

"At 6:00 this morning, the Soviet News Agency, Tass, did what it was told to do and reported that Gorbachev was ill and had temporarily authorized Vanayev to assume the powers of his office. Also, at the very same time, at 6:00 A.M., military commanders were called in and given the same line and ordered to be ready to meet left wing protestors with all necessary force in order to maintain law and order."

"Further, the committee has announced that it will rule by decree for six months. All newspapers with the exception of a few pro-coup rags have been ordered to stop publishing, political parties have been suspended, and any protest demonstrations banned."

"My God, Ned, my God!" Vladimir responded, while putting his head between his hands as he bent forward as if to vomit with mental anguish.

"The last information I have is the worst, my dear friend," he spoke in a deadly tone of voice which sounded like a tomb of a voice.

"The Vitebskaya has their orders, they're being called up and put on alert at this moment."

Ned didn't need to inform Vladimir what the Vitebskaya, the elite KGB airborne division, was called to do: to do what they were ordered to do, to carry out the order of the KGB.

"I'll drive around in my journalist friend's Volvo with his Swedish press credentials and find out whatever else I can," Ned announced, as he arose to unlock the door.

"I'll find you through Katharina," he commented as an afterthought, "she's waiting for you outside".

How typical, he almost responded, of Ned to use an afterthought for leaving him at a loss for thought afterwards. Also, how typical it was for him to be driving a Volvo. Despite or because of the uneasiness of not knowing what might happen next, Vladimir let his mind drift back to what he could so easily predict about Ned. Namely, Ned would never drive a car other than a Volvo, in driving the safe and moral way as he would explain it to anyone and everyone. When they were graduate students at Albany, he called his Volvo the safe car in explaining how it saved his life in a car accident. Later, Ned referred to his Volvo as the moral car in referring to Volvo's refusal to accept a low cost contract from China based on no cost prison labor.

In looking back, Vladimir would have liked to drive off like Ned, in a safe and moral way. He knew, however, that such a drive was only possible in a Volvo. In looking ahead, he had no such choice of driving away, but only the choice of how to drive ahead in fulfilling his mother's vision. Safety can never lead to freedom even if freedom makes one safe. In not being free, one cannot think of safety, and before driving a safe Volvo he'd have to drive his T 72 tank to freedom.

CHAPTER EIGHT

Katharina, His Free Lover

Katharina Yeutushenko had been his lover for four years, ever since they'd met at a peace conference coordinated by Professor Ned Scott as a peacebroker for bringing together East and West in the neutral territory of Sweden on the Baltic island of Gotland. She was a high school teacher like his wife, but unlike his wife she cared about everything and was afraid of nothing. He remembered watching her from a distance during the entire week of the conference hesitant to do more than to admire her without risk from afar. He discovered that she was like himself a Muscovite, all the more reason to keep a respectful distance from what could become too close to home and too close for comfort. Yet, while he felt drawn to this woman with her high yet soft voice, he questioned himself and reminded himself that even though she appeared to be heaven sent, he would be a fool to rush in where angels and comrades fear to tread.

He'd been nominated as a delegate to the World Parliament for Peace, as it was officially designated by the Swedish authorities as a representative of glasnost and perestroika from the Soviet military. Due to his long and close association with Ned, who had submitted his name to the Soviet Union though the circuitous route of the Swedish organizers, he was well prepared to assume a role as a peacekeeper, peacemaker or peacebuilder that other officers in the military could only pretend at.

All week he'd been debating with himself whether it was to be or not to be; it being his approach to her as something more than a fellow peacemaker, as something more like a peacemate. At 8:00 every morning when she'd arrive to take her seat, he would take notice of yet another detail about her from her light smooth skin, to her fine long blond hair, to her dark blue eyes, to her long shapely legs, to . . . . . Yes, he noticed everything about her and to give himself credit, he congratulated himself on how well he concealed it . . . or so he thought. Only recently, she confided to him that she knew exactly every detail about herself that he'd been taking note of, and that she'd decided to pretend to ignore him while taking note of

33

his nervous fumbling around her as awkwardly cute antics for her amusement.

What a most unfortunate modern anomaly between the sexes in both Russia and America that the male is expected to be aggressive and equal with equal contradiction, whereas only the female is allowed to be aggressively equal without contradiction.

In any event, he finally summoned enough courage on the last day of the conference to approach her. She'd been nominated as the Moscow representative of the International Teachers for Peace, in addition to which she represented the Children's Relief Project to provide assistance to children suffering from environmental pollution. Trying to strike the right balance between equality and acceptable aggression, he approached her and asked, "Where are your plans?"

"Major Lubyanka," she responded looking at his name tag and rank at that time, "what plans might you be referring to?"

"To your most important plans," Mrs. Yeutushenko.

"Since you're so direct, Major, may I be so direct as to ask you why you're so interested in my plans?"

"Because I'm interested in you," he responded, relieved at last to be at last honest after sounding so awkwardly blunt.

"Well, well, reporting to a Major on such a matter is somewhat irregular, even, as you might say in the military, out of order, don't you think?" she replied, with a smile expressing both amusement and interest.

"I'm sorry if I've bothered you," he self consciously blurted out, interpreting her apparently dismissive smile as her dismissal of his less than polished approach.

"I am most definitely bothered by something about you", she spoke, as he blushed and looked for a way to extricate himself from his embarrassment.

"And what that is, is that I don't know what the V. stands for on your name tag."

"Vladimir, just call me Vladimir," he smiled to himself and to her.

"And you can just call me Katharina, not Mrs. I'm currently in the process of no longer being a Mrs. You might describe me as the soon to be divorced missing Mrs. who doesn't miss being a Mrs."

"I certainly won't miss that," he responded, in attempting and partially succeeding in giving the desired impression that he wasn't as awkward as he appeared, and that he was almost as genuinely sophisticated as she.

When they arrived back in Moscow he lost no time in rushing in where comrades fear to tread in becoming her lover - her peacemate, her playmate and her soul mate.

What good fortune, he thought to himself, to have a wife who did everything for his career and a lover who did everything for him. His good fortune soon turned to something, else, however, to something better yet more dangerous... to love. As soon as he slept with her, from the first time they became playmates, he discovered that there was no end to what had begun so playfully. No sooner had he finished having sex than he learned that love is never finished. He had all of her and still wanted and needed a never ending more. With her, everything was better and everything was worse: better because there was always more to get and worse because there was always more to give.

She looked far younger than her 35 years, as he looked at her standing across the street in front of the park waiting for him. This was a time of the greatest expectations for him and her, and it seemed to him that the most momentous decisions and the greatest moments in life from the prophetic hope of Vincent Sullivan to the prophetic vision of his mother were ones accompanied by expectation. Even more than figuring out the right answer to the right question - which he had done in deciding that he was a man first and a military man second - knowing what to expect from another seemed to be the ultimate question to which the ultimate answer was knowing what to expect from oneself. The difference he could see clearly as he recalled his mother's vision between hope and despair, the prophetic and the pathetic, is expectation.

He was in love with Katharina but he was obliged to love his wife. With his wife, Raisa, he always expected what he found and found what he expected. With Katharina, he found that what one expects in love is never love. He felt completely free and totally safe with her love, but like his love for his country he knew that in his expectation of her love, freedom can lead to safety but safety can never lead to freedom.

His love for his lover, his promise to his mother, his duty to his country, his responsibility to his men, and his obligation to his wife all rested in his expectation of what he discussed with Ned 20 years before as to what was right and wrong. Most significantly, he noticed that his love for her was first and his concern about what was absolute in terms of what was right or wrong about freedom was last. At this moment in time, his moment of timeless truth, he had to act on what was absolutely right in love and freedom with no time left.

Trying to save time, he ran towards her and stumbled to the ground. As he quickly got back on his feet, he realized how quickly a man runs in love but stumbles to love. He remembered how cautious and hesitant he was to approach her when they first met, sensing, even then, how one may easily run to love but never from it.

She ran up to him and threw herself in his arms asking him, "Are you hurt, are you alright my dear?"

I'm alright, I'm fine," he responded reassuringly, knowing that, indeed, he was fine and that being with her was absolutely all right no matter how absolutely wrong they might be judged by others.

"I'll pick up your things," she stated, as she bent over to retrieve his wallet, car keys and other personal items that had fallen out of his pockets onto the street.

As he put his hands in his empty pockets to see what was missing, he gazed at her while she gathered the loose change on the ground and realized what was absolutely right: that one can be emptied of love but only filled by it.

"Come my dear, I had to be with you before I go," she stated, as she put her arm around his waist after putting his belongings back into his pocket and started to walk with him into the park.

"Go where?"

"To the Russian Parliament, I've helped bring together some people, one or two hundred at most, who will listen to and support Yeltsin. We're meeting in an hour at the Barrikadnaya Metro Station and walking together down Konyuschovskaya Street to our Russian White House.

What an ominously prophetic place to meet, he thought to himself, the Barricade Metro Station.

"Katharina, the whole city is saturated with troops and more are coming in every hour. There could be, in fact, there definitely will be trouble."

"I know that, and Yeltsin's advisors whom I've met with this morning know that as well. In fact, Vladimir, when Yeltsin speaks out against this coup, which he'll do at 12:30, today, when I and a few others will be there to support him, this could be the end."

"Or the beginning of the end," he responded, verbalizing his mother's vision of this day, the day of her own death, being the first of three days in Russia's rising from her old death to a chance of a new life, a new chance at freedom.

"I wanted to be with you now, and to see you one more time in case this should be our last time together," she leaned on him, as they continued to work through the Park, starting to cry uncontrollably.

How easy it is, he reflected, to be controlled by love but how difficult it is to control love.

He felt like berating her for her personal disregard of her own safety but said nothing rather than speak to her, the woman he loved, in the same precautionary way that his wife had spoken to him in the guise of lovingness. He held her and kissed her, still saying nothing but feeling everything and, finally, seeing the difference between lovingness and love between loving and being in love. He had a loving relationship with his wife because he felt he had to, but he was in love with Katharina because he was able to feel what he had. He could be loving to his wife, knowing he should; but he could not but love Katharina, knowing he shouldn't.

Knowing that he shouldn't but that he would, they went to an isolated area of the park surrounded by bushes and trees and kissed, first caressing, then grabbing, then clutching each other for what might remain of their time together instinctively falling to the ground making love. Oblivious to their surroundings and despite and because of the imminent danger, using his overcoat as a mattress, he entered her. He visualized all the other times he'd made love, most vividly their most recent visit to Gotland, the scene of their first awkward encounter four years ago. Counting himself less awkward with each encounter, he'd managed to return with her to that lovely vacation island, situated half way in the Baltic Sea, the Sea of Peace, between the Baltic States and Sweden, for the last three summers.

He clearly recalled boarding the huge Swedish ferry, the Gotlander, which regularly transported tourists back and forth from Germany, Finland and mainland Sweden to Gotland. There were very few if any Russians outside of themselves, since the cost of a week's vacation on Gotland exceeded the average Russian's total annual income. Katharina inherited Scandinavian looks from her north German ethnic ancestry on her mother's side, whereas Vladimir could pass for a central European or a southern German. While the Germans were somewhat resented, more so by the Swedes than the Balts for their unmannerly manner of drawing attention to themselves and even more so for their possessions the most prized of which were their high speeding automobiles, the Russians, he knew, were hated throughout the Baltic States for good reason. Maybe, he reflected, there are no good reasons for something as bad as hate, and the hate haters are right in hating hate. Nevertheless, the Balts had good reason to hate the Soviets for taking advantage of World War II to take over their Baltic States.

Accordingly, while they were both content to be mistaken for anything other than what they were; nevertheless, they looked forward to a day when they could be proud to be recognized, as Russians, for what they were.

Just four weeks before in July, they'd spent two weeks together for the third summer in a row at a cottage located three miles north of Visby, the capital of Gotland, a city of 35,000 inhabitants, inhabited by over 300,000 during the summer months. They arrived as usual on the overnight Gotlander ferry and cruise ship at 7:00 in the morning and took breakfast at a portside cafe located approximately 300 yards from the ship's dock.

Unfortunately, neither of them had been able to sleep on the eight hour voyage due to the noise and commotion caused by too many Swedes and Finns who *Finnished* themselves with too much alcohol. This seemed to be the almost inevitable fate of Scandinavia cruise ships and ferries, one that they'd experienced on each trip to Gotland.

The Russians certainly had more than their share of problems with alcohol; but whereas they might dance and the Germans might sing with their drinks, the Finns and Swedes would invariably sit alone drinking until they collapsed or *Finnished* their drinking bouts with fighting bouts. For some strange reason, the French, who had a far higher per capita alcohol consumption rate than the Swedes, could drink in such a way that you never ran into a drunken Frenchman, whereas your all too often found yourself having to run away from a drunken Swede.

In any event, in vino non veritas, in there being nothing good about being drunk, they found themselves tired but relieved to be off the ship and away from the Soviet Union on their way to their hideaway, Villa Mura Maris. They rented two bikes as they'd done each summer and began the 20 minute assent up the medieval streets of the old town to the castle on the plateau above. Not bothering to rest, they peddled three miles south passing a Volvo garage and a new hotel condominium complex on the left a mile beyond which there was a barely discernable small hand painted sign, Villa Mura Maris, pointed to a dirt road on the left. They coasted down the embankment 100 yards to a partially open white gate that, as always, appeared more designed and positioned to entice people inside than to keep them out.

Even though it was not quite 8:00 a.m., the gardener, as he had for the last two summers, was there waiting for them and ready to help them settle in. He led the way to their cottage, theirs in the sense that they always stayed in the last cottage with the best view located farthest from the Villa's main house and closest to the sea. Thereupon, he opened the unlocked the door and proudly displayed the addition of two new carpets which he himself had just recently installed.

The cottage, about the same size as a medium size American home, contained numerous sculptures created by artists who'd been granted the coveted privilege of staying and working at the Villa. The owner of this 19th century Italian renaissance estate was a reclusive multi millionaire Swedish businessman who purchased it seven years ago from a retired art professor, and who was in the process of renovating the grounds and buildings.

The Villa's three story main house had immense stone roof slates in need of repair and repositioning, which task alone would cost over $250,000.00. The owner, Lars Lundstrum, was rich enough to prevent the Villa from becoming a rich haven for the rich and infamous - usually one and the same - by keeping it as a safe haven for artists and peace activists. Katharina was given free use of the grounds and facilities of the estate for two weeks at the peak of the summer as an expression of his gratitude for her work in the peace movement. For reasons of his own, he liked to have unlikely people working together for peace at his Villa.

Katharina had met the reclusive demi-billionaire at a peace conference in Bycerubsia organized by the International Peace Associates some six years before. Although well into his seventies, Lundstrum was still a business dynamo who'd been able to cut through the maze of the Soviet bureaucracy by cutting out the Party's red tape in arranging business deals for his companies, of which there were more than a dozen. Taking advantage of Swedish neutrality, he'd been able to go East where the rest of the West couldn't go. Taking advantage of peace movements, he orchestrated a go-go refrain for himself and a no-go requiem for his competitors as his business monopoly game with Soviet *officialdumb*. The more unlikely and even unlikable people came together for peace at Villa Mura Maris, the more he liked the profits his business would likely amass. He was very good at making a profit from the Soviets no matter what Marx said about the masses and massive profits.

The Villa, therefore, served a purpose beyond the esthetic one of art, although Lundstrum, unlike most wealthy American patrons of the arts who do little more than patronize the arts, truly appreciated and understood real art. Accordingly, there was no Foundation for the Arts artistes at Villa Mura Maris, only real artists.

The gardens surrounding the estate gave one the impression that they'd been designed for and to the order of a Roman Emperor - majestic and in perfect order from the rows and columns to the statues and fountains. When Ned first organized one of his peace conferences there, he was astonished, as an American, to discover that there was no security for this estate, just a gardener who locked the doors when he left at the end of the day. He remembered Ned's comment that in America the culture of poverty is the poverty of culture; and he contrasted it to the Villa and to Europe in general where art was part of culture and culture was part of the people. Too bad that in America, Vladimir sadly reflected, there's little of culture or art, just the pretense of both for those with plenty of money. Perhaps, that's why art is less likely to be vandalized in a country like Sweden, since common people there are less likely to vandalize what they see as commonly theirs, their part of themselves.

Villa Mura Maris was really the perfect place for Vladimir and Katharina to be. Everyone from the gardener to the occasional visitor, who accepted the open invitation of the partially opened gate to roam the grounds, was real with nothing to hide or hide from. What was most perfect was that it gave the two of them the opportunity to really face each other without hiding from others or from what they felt for each other. It was truly a hideaway rather than a hideout in that they could get away from hiding and get out from hiding from themselves.

Each morning Katharina would prepare breakfast while he picked flowers from the nearby forests to put on the tables. Although they'd both been educated in the equality of the sexes, dogmatically so according to the Marxist-Leninist equality of men and women as comrades, they had forgotten about Marx and Lenin. She relished the chance to be more than a sexual partner and comrade, in being much more than just an equal, in being a real woman. Compared to most of the women he'd met, in both Russia and America, she was a conspicuously wonderful exception to the Soviet Olga the vulgar prototype of feminism – in being wonderfully feminine. Her femininity was neither of the clinging vine nor femme fatale variety but, rather, one of total feminine emotion that left him clinging to her in avoiding the one and only fatal finality for him - life without her.

While making love to Katharina on the improvised ground cloth of his military overcoat underneath the park bushes, his mother's vision grew stronger and stronger the more he pushed inside her. It seemed as if he were experiencing a mystical orgasm wherein God the mother, his mother and Mother Russia, had begotten her only begotten democratic daughter, Katherine, so that Vladimir, the military prodigal son, could see the light of the Russia house and come home to save it and be saved by it. The third person left out of this Female Godhead was the person of the Holy Ghost and that person, Vladimir could now see, was Ned Scott. He was the holistic ghost of a friend who always turned up in upper rooms and other unlikely places when he was least expected and most needed with the whole story. Ned had brought Katharina and him together in the first place, and he'd brought them together, now, in what could be their last place.

He remembered one statement that Katharina made at Villa Mura Maris and he would remember it until the end of their lives - no matter how long or how soon that might be - that freedom in love is not the same as freedom to love. That was all she said when he told her that he loved her, and it left him wondering what she meant by it and it left him wondering what he meant by love. They were equal in the best way a man and a woman can be equal and that is in love. Both of them were in love with each other and both of them knew it, and they were both ready to die for freedom. Yet, he didn't know the right connection between the two, between love and freedom. He saw his love and freedom as right without seeing a right way to connect them.

The hell with right and wrong as some kind of absolute idea fixed in time and place, making love to her was absolutely right for him and for her, so why worry about taking it. Anything good has to be taken, he thought to himself, and since the days of receiving free manna from heaven were gone with the Old Testament desert wind, he would take his freedom in every way: with her, with his men, with his country and maybe, somehow, with his wife. He sounded brave to himself except when it came to his wife, the one person who made him shrink back and shiver, not in fear, but in guilt.

Continuing to make love, thinking back to Villa Mura Maris and thinking ahead to what was now the present future and the future present, he came to the conclusion that if he were going to be free for others, he would first have to be totally free for himself. He decided that before facing others, before risking his life in the cause of his freedom and theirs, he would first have to risk something of his life in facing his life with his wife. He didn't know this because of what he knew or thought he knew about right and wrong. He knew it because he felt it when he made love to the only woman with whom he found real love in finding what was real in love.

Why are love and freedom so God damn complicated, he asked himself, when making love to her and feeling so free, is so God awfully simple? He stopped to correct himself realizing that the common God damn expletive is not just a blasphemy against God, but something far worse, a lie about God, for God doesn't damn us, rather, we damn ourselves in the name of God. Therefore, he corrected himself and began again. Why are love and freedom so People damn complicated, when making love is so God wonderfully simple?

Who do those who talk so much about what's right seem to be the same ones who do so much that's wrong. This coup, he realized, was just one more example in man's long sorry history - his story and her story, mankind's story - of being far less than sorry for doing what's wrong in the name of what's right. This *Moscoup* was just the latest symptom of the epidemic in all systems that legislate might as right - of committing the greatest evil in the name of the greatest good, of destroying life in the literal and figurative inversion of to live which creates an evil spell: the spelling of evil.

This latest attempt to reestablish security and stability, to bring back law and order was a secular Salvationist and Communist version of the one and the same *Pharistocitic* self-righteousness in the secular and religious aristocracies of man. They all centered upon the centric force at the center of all evil of enforcing absolute right answers as final solutions. Final solution, indeed, in its full sinister connotation and historical implication is most apt in describing what Vladimir had to face up to in order to live today, lest he turn away and have it face him down tomorrow.

The answer to the dilemma - past, present and future - of why so much wrong is proclaimed in the name of right, of why so much evil is done in the name of good, of why so many final solutions of death are imposed by those with new manifestos of life is that their absolutely right answers proceed from absolutely wrong questions.

The coup started with the absolutely wrong question of how to establish their law and their order, of *justus* over justice, to which

Vladimir had his own absolutely right question - if not yet a right answer - the question of not only how to take one's freedom but how to take one's freedom without taking others.

Sometime, soon, he'd know the right answer to any question about love and freedom, but, at this moment, he would give the right answer to any question she might have about his love for her in continuing to have her come again and again.

He visualized being back at their cottage and how much fun they'd had every morning after breakfast trying to land navigate themselves through the serpentine path in the forest descending almost cliff like along the steep hills down to the water. This narrow forest path was so similar to the Iroquois Indians warpath trail along a cliff from the forest situated on a high plateau down to Seneca Lake in Upstate New York that he wondered whether perhaps the Vikings had brought some Iroquois Indians to Gotland on their return from an ancient seafaring expedition to North America.

Upon returning to the cottage after their morning swim, they would make love as they looked out the long, high and wide artists window - a window made by and for artists - that gave them a window on the world at its idyllic best. There was a view of the sun and the surf, the green sea and the blue sky, the stone cliffs and the pebble beach, the grand ocean going ships and the small fishing boats, a view that allowed him to view himself from outside as he viewed her from inside.

Looking at himself from outside, he saw a man with apparently the best of both worlds: a wife who supported his career and a lover who supported him. Few men from the bottom ring of society were fortunate enough to marry into a family whose position could propel their career upwards; and few men in any society could boast of a lover such as Katharina who could propel them upward in every way. Yes, indeed, he certainly appeared to be the man who had it all and he did have it all, but others could not see all the guilt that he also had.

While Katharina gave all of herself to him, he gave all that he could of himself to her. The part that he could not give belonged to his wife, to their twenty years together, to his successful career, to his military security, to their political stability, and to the safety of their life together. Ever since meeting Katharina, he took his freedom in loving her and, as a result, he found himself less free with his wife and less sure of everything else in his life.

Freedom may be an absolute right as almost anyone today, faithless Fidel excluded, would tell you. But no one tells you that the price of freedom is never free. There are a few bad-old-boys left, like the coup plotters, who try to deny freedom in a last desperate grab at control. And there are a few middle aged, middle of the road reformers like Gorbachev, who try to rationalize rationing freedom as a controlled substance with prescribed doses. They're both doomed, nevertheless, to terminal illness in a futile attempt to compromise with freedom.

Freedom cannot be controlled, prescribed or compromised with rationalized and rationed reforms. Freedom comes from the soul, and with one's soul rationalization is irrational and rationing is a short fall ratio that can never go far enough for one can never ration one's soul.

Just as Gorbachev was taken hostage because he tried to have the best of both political worlds, Vladimir felt himself taken hostage by trying to have the best of both loving and love relationships, the best of both Raisa and Katharina. Instead of becoming freer to have both, however, he felt less free to have either in becoming more and more in bondage to the slavery of his own freedom.

How ironic that the more rationalization and compromise with freedom in political life, the more hostage taking; and how even more ironic that the more freedom in taking the best of two women who love you, the more you're taken hostage by yourself. How ironically absurd it is, either we as human beings are absurd or else our ideas about love and freedom are absurd, or just maybe the whole people-damn world and all its personal and political ideas are absurd.

Yet, absurd as it may be, he knew there was no escape from it all and no way away from his freedom to love or risk losing love, to stay safe at home or risk losing the safety of a home, to have real freedom or a false peace with Katharina, Raisa, his country and himself. Ned had always told him that love and freedom are always absolute but never fixed. Yes, Ned, he knew, was right, but, even so, where are you if you know something's right, absolutely right, but you don't know where it is in yourself. If he could find out, better yet, if he could like his mother see it, then everything else would work out and nothing would be absurd anymore.

There were two questions that he had to answer at this moment of choice and vision, what to do for himself and what to do for others. He closed his eyes, while resting inside Katharina, as he saw his mother's vision of Mother Russia rise to his own personal situation and present circumstance of choice. In reference to himself, he saw that he could heal himself by love but never from love; and in reference to others, he saw that a false peace at the price of real freedom is a false freedom at the price of real peace. The bridge between the two was one of finding a way to take one's freedom without taking others freedom away.

Now he could also see what Katharina meant by saying to him that to be free in love is neither love nor freedom, in response to which he could see that to be free to love is both love and freedom. Perhaps it was wrong to make love to a woman other than his wife, but it was better to love in sin than to sin in love. He loved Katharina and he loved freedom and he could see the direction he had to go in order to go and sin no more - to liberate himself and others.

The first direction would be to Raisa, to face the risk of facing his life and to risk what had been the sum total of his life with her.

"Katharina, before I go to my base… I'm going home," he hesitated, in sounding as if he no longer had a home.

"I understand, Vladimir, you have to choose, but I love you no matter what you choose."

Those were the exact same words that she sung out to him on their last day together at Villa Mura Maris in her own improvised rhapsody in the rain. They awoke that morning to a torrential downpour and decided that instead of taking a shower inside, they'd avail themselves of the gift of nature's shower outside in making love in her downpour. Since they were in Sweden, they didn't even care if one of the resident artists might see them or if a visitor came by to get out of the rain. In that respect, the Swedes were somewhat of an innocuous anomaly that made them more difficult at times to understand than even the Americans, who were far from innocuous.

Making love in the rain, even swimming nude at an American beach would get one arrested. The puritan heritage is a strong influence in both America and Sweden, the difference being that the Americans react with cultured excess and personal hypocrisy, whereas the Swedes split morality into public and private spheres with sex relegated to a morally marginal but categorized imperative.

In America, personal morality of a schizophrenic do your own thing but pretend you don't variety is substituted for public morality such that, as evidenced by the variety of public scandals, public morality becomes a morality play with a variety of amoral public players. In effect, there is no public morality and in its place a person's private morality becomes paramount to the degree that it becomes part of Paramount casting. From Presidential aspirant Gary Hart's, you've got to have heart, heart to heart escapades, to someone else's abortion becoming everyone else's business, private morality replaces public morality.

In Sweden, cheating the public by means of tax evasion is considered a moral capital offense. In America, however, the same deed is not only widely practiced but, indeed, highly valued with entire professions of lawyers and accountants becoming wealthy through their expertise of legal cheating. The Swedes tend to abuse alcohol more than Americans and have more sex than Americans, who prefer to talk much more about sex and create abusive expressions and gestures with which to express their peculiar frustrations with it. While the Swedes regulate personal excess with excessive taxation, the Americans deregulate cultural excesses most in evidence in places like Salt Lake City, Utah and Las Vegas, Nevada.

Vladimir recalled a university spring vacation tour out West for international students, as part of which two days were spent in Salt Lake City and the following two in Las Vegas. He remembered the cultural extremes and excesses between these two tourist destinations as being truly bizarre and most illustrative of the puritanical - libertine schizophrenia of America. In Salt Lake City, nothing was available (he wondered if Mormon polygamy might still be responsible for women hoarding) not even a beer; whereas in Las Vegas, everything was available 24 hours a day to include not only gambling, women and alcohol, but a ride in Adolph Hitler's personal armored limousine . . . Wow!? Although Vegas did have some normal entertainment, the main reaction Vladimir had was one of astonishment at the extent to which bad taste could become good business in America.

Making love in a downpour had an exquisite taste about it that left him reeling with a feeling of joy unparalleled by that of a ride in Adolph's limo. When she began to sing out through the rain dripping down her face that she loved him, he knew it meant everything; whereas if it had happened in Vegas, he doubted it would mean anything. The Swedes, even more than the Americans with their sin taxes, had a long history of heavy personal taxes on pleasure. Indeed, this Swedish puritanical anomaly did worry him, for if they were to tax him for his personal pleasure in the rain, he'd never get out of the rain in being bankrupt for the rest of his life.

"I must go home now," he hurriedly spoke, as he hurried to leave in order to do what he must.

"Katharina, you'll see me again today or else you'll never see me again."

"Vladimir, I see something more in your eyes," she whispered, as she gently stroked his hair and looked into his eyes.

"I see that no longer are so you free in love with me."

"Yes, Katharina my dear," he embraced her as they leaned back against the nearby tree, "you never fail to see before I do. You're right about me, I do see more about myself. I see that I'm free to be more than free in love, in being freer to love, more free to love you."

"I don't want to leave you," she stood up as she buttoned her blouse, "but I must leave you now for if I don't, I'll never be able to leave."

"Katharina, I don't want you to leave me either, but if I stopped you, if I pulled you back, you wouldn't be free for yourself and then you couldn't give yourself freely to me."

He bent over to pick up and put on his well used overcoat as she finished dressing. They quickly turned away from each other walking in different directions, afraid to say goodbye and afraid that if either of them looked back their hearts would stop. He drove home even faster than he'd driven to his mother, weaving in and out and around the growing numbers of troop trucks and armored personnel carriers that were still pouring into Moscow. In driving with increasing recklessness, he realized that he was trying to face what he had to, but didn't want to, by speeding away from it all to get it over with as soon as possible. Here he was on the run again, this time from one woman to another driven by the vision of a third woman, his mother, whose vision would keep driving him for the rest of his days and most of all, for the rest of this day.

He once assumed he had plenty of time... time to care for his mother, time to enjoy the comforts of his life with his wife, time to love the woman in his life, time to peacefully retire and time to choose. How we assume so much about what's ours, particularly how much time we have. The only time we can count on is the time to choose. While driving home or, rather, what was once home, he thought to himself that during most of our lives we take too much time or too little: too much time to choose and too little time to decide. We pretend to ourselves that we need more time to choose because we don't want to choose; and we take too little time to decide because we want to think that whatever happens, it happened to us rather than that we made it happen.

Katharina was an exception to this general human rule for she took little time in choosing him and much time in deciding. She chose him when they met after their first awkward encounter at Villa Mura Maris, but only later did she decide to love him. Sex was a quick choice for her. Love, however, was a careful decision because she knew that with precautionary care, sex can be safe, but no matter how careful or cautious, love is never safe. It occurred to him that Russians and Americans are alike in many respects but quite unalike in love and sex. Whereas Americans laugh at love and try to be so serious about sex, Russians take sex as it comes while they're very serious about love.

She'd been married for fifteen years to the perfect man, perfect not only by everyone else's account but perfect in her eyes as well. When she wanted to study further for more teaching degrees, her husband did all the housework so she could do all her homework. When she decided to spend more time away from home in working for the causes of world peace and a better environment, he took up her causes at home and abroad as his own in providing her with every sort of help and support. By any man or woman's measure, he measured up. Without any doubt, he was the perfect husband up and until the very day she decided to leave him.

It took Vladimir a long time to understand this glaring contradiction about her, to find the answer to the question as to why would the perfect woman leave the perfect husband. This dilemma was further complicated for him by the fact that both she and he were well aware that he was far from being the perfect man and, certainly, the last thing from a perfect husband.

The greatest irony among so many human ironies appeared to be the common phenomena of so many women staying with not only imperfect but abusive husbands, while so many others were leaving perfect husbands. He knew from experience that the simple stereotypes about women being emotional and men being logical served as an explanation only for the simple minded. Women were just as logical as men and even more capable of rigorous calculation in engineering human emotions. The answer, then, lied somewhere other than with simplistic sexisms about the sexes. The answer, he later discovered, was even simpler but far more disturbing.

Katharina had married at the age of twenty, right out of her parents' home to her husband's home. In many ways, in fact in all ways, Katharina was a reflection, a beautiful reflection but, nevertheless, a reflection, a reflection of her family - open, trusting and loving. She was good, kind, and intelligent but, above all else, she was a reflection in that she reflected others rather than herself. Her husband, Igor, was slightly older and terribly in love with her, terrible in the sense that love is terrible when it isn't equal. He loved her beauty and her goodness and what she reflected, and he did everything for her so she could find herself and be herself so he could love her even more.

It not only perplexed him but it bothered him that women, and particularly the woman he loved, seemed to act not in an illogical way, as the simple sexists assert, but in a so different way from men. What man would leave the perfect woman he thought to himself and, then, answered himself by looking at himself. Wasn't Raisa in most ways the perfect wife? And, wasn't he about to leave her? Yes, but still, there was a major difference between the sexes, and Katharina was a major illustration of that difference that he was still trying to understand.

He recalled a divorce very similar to Katharina's and Igor's wherein all who knew the couple was shocked because the husband, like Igor, was regarded by everyone including his wife to be the perfect husband. The mother of the woman, a very wise old woman, said something to him that he wanted to forget but never did.

"The worst problem for the best of women is a better husband," she'd stated in all seriousness, and it left him fearing that perhaps one old wise woman was wiser than any three wise men.

Reflecting upon the difference between wise old men and the wise old women, he compared the three Biblical wise men that followed their star to this wise old woman and concluded that the difference goes beyond that of knowledge and vision to the relationship between them. Whereas wise men may follow a vision in following a star, they first must know in order to see; whereas the wise old woman first must see in order to know, for her vision is the start of rather than the star to knowledge.

Her statement made him afraid because if she were correct, and he was afraid she was, then it explained why so many women endure abuse and abandon loving care. The old woman's wise insight to the effect that the worst problem for a perfect woman is a more perfect husband, that the best woman can endure anything except a better husband, explained why Katharina loved him - the fact of which made him rejoice and the explanation for which made him shutter.

Vladimir knew himself and he knew he was neither an exceptionally good man nor an exceptionally bad man, but he knew he was exceptionally strong. Igor was the perfectly perfect, lovingly loving husband, but he was no where near as strong as he was. And this was the reason why she left Igor and came to him. What made him shutter was the realization that even the best of women, in her case the very best of a woman, prefer strength over goodness in men. Men, to the contrary, particularly the very best of men and the very best in a man, prefer goodness over strength in a woman.

He uttered the time worn ending of a retrospective Amen to this difference between men and women. Amen literally means So Be It, although he would have preferred a different ending, a futuristic Be It So, that would allow for change such that both sexes would prefer goodness over strength in each other. Some day, and some day soon, he hoped that the worst equality between men and women, the feminist equality in Olga the Vulgar coarseness, would be replaced with the best equality of goodness. On that day, women would have equal power with men with no need, therefore, to find the right and wrong strength they lack in the opposite sex.

Arriving back at his apartment, he felt less strong as well as less than good with guilt overwhelming any and all other feelings about himself. Katharina overcame her being a reflection of others in reflecting her own freedom to herself to decide what she needed, rather than pretending to need what others needed or decided she needed. She took her own freedom in becoming more than a reflection of her family; more than a feminist reflection, she became her own woman. In the process Igor was devastated, but he still had his freedom which she'd never taken from him. Igor was unlucky in having lost at love, but Vladimir felt more unlucky in having a guilty love. Igor lost his love in being left with his freedom, whereas Vladimir had lost his freedom to love to his wife. Katharina left Igor with the freedom to love again, whereas Raisa left him with neither love nor the freedom to love again without guilt.

He felt immense guilt because he felt that he owed Raisa, that he owed himself to her for all she'd done in advancing his career. She was his marital counterpart to Katharina's husband, Igor, who similarly did everything for her. Whereas Katharina had the courage of her freedom and the freedom of her courage to leave the perfect husband, he felt the tremendous weight and the heavy dumbbell of guilt in finding his courage and freedom to leave the career officer's perfect wife. As he stepped out of his car to walk to his apartment, he glanced up and down the broad avenue looking for an armored personal career with the sudden prospect of doing something to get himself killed. He saw dying as an easier way out than facing and having to live with his guilt.

Luckily, at that instant, there was no APC in sight, and he quickly regained his temporary sanity - temporary in that sanity and insanity are contingent on both what happens to us and what we make happen.

Guilt, contrary to *Fraudian* psychology is the eminently same grim reality of the consequences of our actions, of what we make happen to ourselves; whereas love is a wonderfully insane reality of what we let happen to ourselves, without which our lives become insane. He felt guilt with good reason but he rose to face it because he had love for no good reason, although love was the reason for every good. Love like the irrationality of faith goes beyond good reason as a free gift with a price - the price of one's choice. Like faith, it leads to a final rational choice to irrational need culminating in supernatural good, that of the *chosenness* of God's love. No one can claim it for themselves but everyone can choose it as theirs. The old Amen is an unfree So Be It to being chosen, whereas the new Amen is a free Be It So to having chosen.

It occurred to him that rather than solve any problem, love heals all problems. As he prepared himself to face Raisa, he thought of his lover. Katharina had shown him that while there's an absolute freedom from everything and everyone, there's no absolute freedom to anything or anyone except oneself.

Waiting on the downstairs level before going up to their apartment, as he'd waited just hours before in going to see his dying mother, he once again hesitated to go ahead. In both situations he waited and hesitated before facing death. He first hesitated at the happy death of a mother who knew little but saw everything; and, now, he hesitated at the unhappy death of a marriage to a wife who knew everything and saw nothing.

He would not let his guilt turn him into an emotional coward. He would tell her the truth, but in a way that would cause her the least pain. He would do his best, he would, he said to himself, be very good in telling her what would be very bad for her to hear. Listening to how good he sounded to himself made him think of another human irony of how we react so badly to the do-gooder. The average run of the mill do gooder is perceived as less appealing, in effect less good and more bad, than the average run to the gin mill bad doer.

It's an ironic paradox that doing good should evoke the very opposite reaction of vilifying the do-gooder. Obviously, there's something not so good about doing good, he concluded, as he looked back at Katharina's life and looked forward to the rest of his life. She left a husband who did nothing but good, showering her with a loving goodness, because he smothered her with doing good to her rather than helping her find what was good for her. Vladimir would present the truth to his wife that her loving care and concern for him was another kind of doing good that kept him locked into what she wanted rather than what he needed.

Truth hurts but it doesn't destroy unless one continues to lie to oneself. He would have to summon all his strength to be both truthful in telling her he'd been untrue while doing good in the only way that doing good can really do good: by telling the truth while inflicting the least amount of pain. He would try to be loving at this moment of invoking the truth in setting himself free, in knowing that while lovingness is kind only love heals. Love won't solve others problems or problems with others, but it can heal one's problem with oneself. He would be loving - in the best sense of being kind - while he hurt her with the truth in healing himself by freeing himself to love Katharina. He found an absolute freedom in himself to leave the woman who'd been his wife and career manager for twenty years. He repeated to himself that while there is an absolute freedom from everything and everyone, there is no absolute freedom to anything or anyone, except to oneself. Perhaps the truth might not only hurt, but destroy. And perhaps nothing would be solved by his love, but it was the only choice that would allow him to heal himself and allow his wife the choice of healing herself.

Is it wrong, he asked himself, to feel such guilt at the prospect of leaving Raisa? No, it's not wrong to feel guilt, for guilt can be right or wrong depending on what one's guilty about. Despite the worst of *Fraudian* analysis - he wanted to say best and worst but couldn't think of anything better than the worst - guilt is quite sane and reasonable when you've hurt another. You may have every right to hurt that person, even as in his case, a wife who's been a very good wife or at least the best wife she knew how to be, but that right didn't make him feel all right.

The problem he now could see, as he opened the door of his apartment to face his wife, was not what his wife knew, but what she couldn't see. She was a highly educated Marxist intellectual, the only daughter of a Soviet General and a mother with a Ph.D. in

Marxist studies. Her parents were good parents, in fact too good if it's possible to be bad by being too good - like the bad do-gooder - in that they did everything good to their only child just as she'd done everything good to him as his wife. The problem with her, with her family, and with their Marxism was that while they were constantly trying to correct what was wrong they could never see what was right: the more good they did to others the more bad those others felt.

The result of her family's dedication to Marxism and his wife's dedication to his career was a personal desert inside scorched by the dry heat of too much good being done leaving the recipient thirsty for the chance to do good for himself. He needed to drink the waters - bitter and sweet - of freedom as a good he got for himself rather than a good got done to him by others. Among all peoples there is a universal belief in belief, most of all among unbelievers, who, like the Marxists, in disavowing the belief of other creeds, create their own belief in the collective creed of all good residing in themselves. Therefore, one must beware not only of the true believer as someone who truly believes rather than one who believes in truth; but one must be even more beware of the atheistic believer in his own belief in the goodness of his collective group.

CHAPTER NINE

Raisa, His Communist Wife

As he saw his wife come to him and they embraced, he could see quite intimately that while there are atheists even in foxholes - there are no unbelievers anywhere for everyone believes in something he or she can't be sure of. Raisa believed in her marriage and nothing else, while he believed that there was something else more important to believe in than his marriage. Nevertheless, he didn't want to hurt her and he wanted to leave her with belief in herself.

"Vladimir, my dear, I'm so glad you've come to your senses and came home to me."

"Raisa, please sit down," he spoke, saying to her without saying that he had not come home to her.

"I was with my mother when she died this morning."

"My dear, I'm so sorry, but you shouldn't feel upset about it for she was very old and very ill. Better for her that she passed away now than lived on to die in more pain later."

"Yes, maybe so, but, you know, she taught me a great lesson, she died without pain, she spoke to me as she died with joy and with a vision."

"OK," she responded, prepared to respond to anything other than a vision.

"She left me with her vision, Raisa, and it's no longer just her vision. It's my vision and it's a vision not only for me but for others."

"Oh my God!" she cried out, with an emotional illogic in invoking the name of a deity whose existence she officially disavowed as a member of the Communist Party.

"I'm not going to wait for an order," he asserted. "Instead, I'm going to give myself an order, my personal order to combat this coup!"

"Jesus Christ!" she exclaimed, in horror rather than faith, in seeing the light in her husband's eyes.

"She's done it, your mother has finally done it. She's not satisfied to have lost her husband in a war, no, she's got to make sure on her deathbed that she brings death to her son so he, too, can be remembered as some kind of Russian hero."

"No, that's not it," he responded.

"Yes that is it," she interrupted.

"Your mother never liked me, Vladimir. You know she didn't because unlike you, I was not raised by an impoverished, superstitious woman. I was taught to understand reality, to use science not faith in trying to build a better world. And I have built a better world for you. You must be honest enough to admit that."

"Yes. . ." he tried to continue, as she waited just long enough for his yes to continue her diatribe.

"The day we were married she said something to me about her vision of you returning to her as your dying mother to save a dying Mother Russia. You were her only child, the pride and joy of a woman who lost her husband, and she never accepted you as my husband more than as her son. You were both her son and her husband, her family and her life; and now that her life's over, she wants to make sure that she takes you with her and that your life is over as well!"

"This lesson of hers, this great lesson that you say she taught you is, I agree with you, a lesson alright. It's her final bequeath and requiem, literally, of a lesson, for it leaves a less son, of less of a son. It leaves you with less of everything we've built together, and, in all likelihood, less of your own life in facing a likely death."

"I will not have it, Vladimir, and I will not have you if you go ahead with this insane order of yours. Your order is for you, not for us. I didn't spend twenty years guiding and cultivating Second Lieutenant Vladimir Lubyanka through the ranks to Colonel with more promotions to follow for the sake of being the wife a visionary. You'll die in disgrace even if they don't kill you on the spot, which is not only possible but quite probable as you must know. Vladimir, how can you not know that?"

"I know the risk . . ." once again he could barely start a sentence let along finish it before she'd verbally jump on his words.

"Yes, you know, you say you know, but you don't care! You don't care because your crazy old religious fanatic of a superstitious mother left you with a vision, and some vision at that?" You, one Lieutenant Colonel Vladimir Lubyanka, are going to issue an order to yourself to combat the multi million man armed forces of the Soviet Union in order to rise and save Mother Russia? Don't you realize how crazy that is, how insane it sounds? Have you become suicidal as well as ungrateful after all I've done for you, the son of a widowed peasant, to make you what you are today and can be even more of tomorrow? Have you thought of that, have you, have you, have you?"

She took a few seconds to catch her breath ending her diatribe with tears of anger as Vladimir decided against another futile attempt at responding in allowing her to conclude her crying and continue her diatribe.

"I know you, Vladimir, as your wife I know more about you than even you do, and I warn you that you won't be a Russian hero for a new era or a legend in your own time, a suicidal legend at that. Rather, you're a deluded legend in your own mind throwing away your life in the cause of a new error rather than a new era. Remember what happened at Tiananmen Square! Let me talk to you about that in response to your talking to me about your vision. There were tanks there, also, and they ran over those westernized democratic demonstrators with their American statue of liberty. They crushed them and they toppled their replica of an American statue just as they'll crush and topple any other replica of these alien democratic ideas. Is that how you want your career and your life to end? Do you want to die as a traitor, as a Western agent who used his military training to turn on his own government, in fighting against the very same system that's brought us to the comfortable position we're in?"

"Remember something else my visionary husband, remember how those who died fighting for an American statue of liberty were remembered by the Americans themselves. Remember how the Americans described even by your democratic friends as the unholy Trinity, the Troika of Henry *Kissinkick*, a former Secretary of State who earned his name kissing fat ass and kicking little ass, Brent *Socrafty* and Lawrence *Eataburger* the third helping remembered those demonstrators in Tiananmen Square. They ran to Peking before the blood was even dry on the ground to make sure that the business of corporate and government prison labor would go on as usual. *Kissinkick* kissed fat old Chinese ass as he kicked dead young Chinese ass, while *Socrafty* so craftily made dead meat by *Eataburger's* most favored trade third helping. Probably, your friend Ned Scott will show up at your funeral, but as far as the rest of the West is concerned you're just a little ass for the likes of *Kissinkick* and his ASSociates to Kick ass."

"I know you're upset, Raisa, and it's true what you said about the moral awful *Kissinkick* reflex in the knee jerk cause of *lousey* - faire capitalism. And, maybe, I just might get my little ass kicked, but that doesn't mean I'm going to make it easy for *Kissinkick's* Associates. The best way to protect one's ass is not to sit on it waiting around for others' orders, but to become if necessary and by God its necessary now, a bad ass in fighting for one's own ass. Raisa, I'll admit you're one hundred percent correct about the Tiananmen replica of the American statue of liberty. However, it was bound to fall but not because of personal freedom and political liberty, but because it was someone else's statue of liberty. The lesson to learn from Tiananmen Square is that a fight for your freedom is your fight and no one else's. Freedom can only be won by fighting for one's own personal stature of liberty rather than someone else's statue of liberty."

"We've become different," Vladimir continued to speak, in asserting his right to do so after having waited so long to respond to his wife's accusations. "You, like your military and party family, react to a new era as a new error because for you, living under a known order is always better, even it it's dead wrong, as long as you're comfortable. You'd rather live a dead life with any known old order than risk living with an unknown new order, no matter how necessary and right it may be."

"You're absolutely correct in saying that you've made my career, and always provided very well for us with the best, and always at the expense of the rest. You know what's wrong with you, Raisa, you know what the real problem is with you and with us? It's not what you know for you're very well informed, even more so at many times than I am, but you can't see because you won't see what's right."

AMEN means SO BE IT

"Yes, Raisa, to see, to have vision is the best insight as to what can be and, despite all you know, you don't have any insight or vision. In effect, you're blind with your eyes wide open: You accuse my mother of being a superstitious ignorant peasant mumbling her prayers while she deludes herself and me with her visions. Well, while she may know little compared to all you know, she sees all that can be; whereas you look back at all that has been and see nothing beyond what is. You're a believer as much as she is except you're secular belief closes your eyes while her spiritual belief opens others eyes. Further, you're more an Amen sayer with your commandments for yourself than she is with her vision for others."

"Your Marx was right about religion being used as an opiate of the people except he left out the fact that his quasi religious Manifesto was the worst drug of all. The Communist Manifests is a communist bible and fundamentalist prayer book that ends every one of its beliefs pretending to be facts with its own Amen as an ending to its own prayer. It's an Amen ending of what could be with the Amen of an historically determined SO BE IT. A real prayer, a true vision like my mother's, sees beyond the past and a present determined by the past to a present determination for the future. It's a freely determined Amen of a present and future BE IT SO. I say Amen to your unfree Amen of a deterministic SO BE IT. And I pray Amen with a free BE IT SO vision of having determined, of having chosen, rather than of having been determined, of having been chosen."

That's the difference between your Marxist prayer book compared to my mother's prayer, and its vision and prayer for me. You and I both pray, but in so doing we look in opposite directions. You look back and I look forward. You look to just you and me, to just us, to your *justus*; whereas I look to what's right and just not just for us but for others as well - to justice for all of us."

"I'm not some deranged suicidal fanatic trying to die a martyr's death. I'm not some soldier of God who loves death; rather I'm a soldier of God who loves what's right. I believe its right to believe in a God of right, who loves life and freedom. Further, I'm going to practice what I preach - in teaching the practice of freedom by my example. I'm going to fight for freedom, my freedom, and your freedom - even if you can't see it. Finally, I'm going to fight for my country's freedom and fight for a world at peace with freedom."

"I don't believe in laying down my life for another," he spoke with a depth of emotional calm to match the depth of his wife's emotional hysteria, "but in picking it up for others."

"Those others will see, and when they see my personal order for me, they'll see themselves differently. They'll fight not at my order or others orders, or for an old or new world order, but they'll fight because of my order as their order for themselves.

"For all of our life together, I was your career officer husband on the way up. Now, for the first time in our 20 years together, I'm a man, first, on the way up, at last, to becoming a free man. To you, it's a way down and out, but to me it's the only way to be a man. I don't want to continue to be your Lieutenant Colonel of a husband, who can order others. Instead, I prefer that you Just Call Me Vladimir, a man who can order himself for others to follow in freedom, and to follow to freedom."

"It's your choice, Raisa, did you marry a rank, an up and coming Lieutenant Colonel or a man called Vladimir, an upstart who's starting to face any and all comers in the coming era of freedom? You choose! When I came back here I was prepared for this to be my decision, but it's also yours. Here's my rank, I'm taking it off and giving it back to you because it's yours. Here it is, and it's rightfully yours for twenty years of loving care for me as your military investment for your rank marriage. It's just you and I, now, like it was in the beginning. Are you still my wife or not?"

"So that's it, at last you've really put yourself last. That's what I get for all these years of loving you, of providing for you, of taking care of your career… an ultimatum. Well, Vladimir, as you just prefer to be called, you're no longer a Lieutenant Colonel. In fact, you're no longer anybody but a soon to be dead body. You have your pie in the sky vision and I, no thanks to your God, have my clear vision that your mother's visionary insight is your suicidal blindsight; and, now, I want you out of my sight! I'll have nothing from here on out to do with you. I'm going to call the Interior Minister, Boris Pugo, and the General Chief of Staff, Marshall Sergei Akhromeyev, and immediately inform both the political and military authorities that, as of today, we're no longer together. And I, hereby, divorce myself from you and every action you're taking."

"I'm sorry for you, and I'll just call you Vladimir," she sneered as she spoke, "the soon to be late who might have been great Lieutenant Colonel Lubyanka, for I thought you'd know better."

He turned to leave and then turned back to say, "I'm sorry for you, Raisa, for I thought you might have been able to see better."

As he left his comfortable apartment and his wife behind forever, he saw that indeed there was an ultimatum that they'd given to each other. Better than being lovingly kind to one another, they'd been brutally honest to each other; and there was, now, no way back to their life together. She saw his vision as a pie in the sky death wish, while he saw it as life over death and as more than a wish. For him it was a living order for his life over death to take the pie of freedom from the sky above and personally bring it down to his earth below.

How ironic, he thought to himself, as he got into his car for the twenty five mile drive to his base that she used the word ultimatum to describe what he was saying. What she said made him realize that they'd reached the end of their marriage in an ultimatum to each other precisely because there was no ultimate presence between them. If they'd had an ultimate quality in their marriage from the beginning, there would never have been an ultimatum in their marriage at the end.

Once again, he could see the immense gap and unbridgeable chasm between lovingness and love. While love is ultimate, lovingness eventually succumbs to or issues ultimatums. Where love creates freedom, lovingness creates control in the name of love and in the place of freedom. He could see the clear difference between the two because he could see Katharina in comparison to Raisa. Katharina loved him in an ultimate way and they were free to love without any ultimatums, whereas Raisa had been loving towards him in lovingly controlling his freedom. Raisa was loving to him, whereas Katharina's love was for him. Katharina left her husband and he left his wife because they both left ultimatums of lovingness about freedom for the ultimate freedom to love.

Now that he'd faced his moment of truth about love and freedom in being free to love Katharina and to speak the truth with Raisa, he could better face the moment of truth with his men. For the first time he'd face them as just Vladimir rather than as their commanding officer Lieutenant Colonel Lubyanka. He knew there'd be call ups as he rushed to the headquarters of the Tamanskaya Guards Division to issue the first call, the first order to himself as a call to them to call up to their conscience rather than crawl down to the coup.

He stopped the car and went to a phone booth to call Ned at the home of the Swedish journalist and luckily he was there.

"Ned, I need to know everything that's happened and I need to know it right away!"

"I'll meet you," Ned responded, in shouting into the phone above the noise of the static, "on the side of the road in a blue Volvo near the last building before you approach the main gate of the Guards Division at 2:15."

He hung up and looked at his watch. It was 12:30, exactly the time Katharina said she'd be at the Russian Parliament, the ad hoc democrat's white house, supporting the Russian President, Boris Yeltsin.

CHAPTER TEN

Yeltsin As Yell Sin

Yeltsin, he thought, what an appropriately politically prophetic name for a man who would have to yell about the sins of the coup, to yell sin to those handful of visionaries with Katharina in order to save not only Russia, but the world. Perhaps Russian President Boris Yeltsin was a political bull in a diplomatic china shop, but at least he didn't drop China in selling out the Chinese democrats as did the Bush league. Yeltsin dropped everything, including his personal safety to protest the *coupspiracy*. In contrast, *Kissinkick's* drop in to drop by Tiananmen with a drop dead *coupspirit* of 'Me thinks Chinese students protest too much' drop kick was a dead drop coup against the spirit of freedom. Russia, the world, and most of all the Americans, after turning their deaf ear to the Balts, needed to hear Yeltsin, the Russian bear of a prophet.

Yeltsin could Yell Sin better than any prophet at any freedom revival anywhere in making a new name for himself as the Prophet Yellsin. He yelled sin for all to hear, in baring the sins of Communism, in calling all to repent with a penitential refrain of freedom for all.

At the very least, Yeltsin, in yelling about the sins of the coup, would give others a chance to make a choice in finding their way to freedom. No longer would he refer to Boris as just Yeltsin. Instead, with the greatest admiration for his stand, he would forever hereafter refer to him as Boris the Yellsin. To a televised world evangelized by the bore of a Jim and Tammy Bakering verbal diarrhea, and a boring Jim Swaggering whoring in preaching fire and brimstone from on high, Boris Yellsin would bore in on the sins of the *coupspirasin*. He took his televised place in history on the podium of a tank, boring away at the sins of the *coupspiracy*. He delivered his most powerful freedom sermon in preaching Russia's white, blue and red fire and brimstone, in exorcising a red too hot to touch hammer and sickle with the hammer of freedom's fiery opposition from below.

The main streets and squares were blocked by tanks, APCs, troop trucks and jeeps as Vladimir finally found his way away from Moscow to the outskirts of the city driving twenty five miles west off the main highway to Minsk. He arrived at exactly 2:15 pm to find Ned waiting for him in a blue Volvo with Swedish news plates at their designated meeting place a quarter mile distant from the main entrance to the headquarters of the Tamanskaya Guards Division. He pulled behind the Volvo and got inside to find out what he would have to know before he could talk with rather than to his tankers, the men he'd commanded for over a decade. For the first time in his military life which had been his life, he realized that any future order for his life would have to be a right order. It would have to be right not in being a clear and certain order from outside, but right in his certainty about the rightness of a personal order from what's clearly inside.

"Holy Ghost, Vladimir," Ned spoke turning pale, "I thought you'd look different, but you're actually smiling. I never expected to see you smiling at a time like this."

"My good friend, you were expecting a ghost of a man and instead you're looking at me white as a ghost. Have you forgotten, when you were a soldier, how we must be able to smile in the face of death?"

"No, I remember, but I also remember how easy it was for so many to say it and how very few, if any, could ever do it. I can see you're one of those very few."

"I may be one of those very few and, possibly, I may be the only one, but soon there'll be others, even if only a few others. Ned, you were more correct than perhaps you intended in calling me Holy Ghost. I'm looked upon as a ghost by Raisa, and almost everyone else thinks I don't have a ghost of a chance. In fact, she's left me because of it."

"Because of what?" Ned inquired.

"Because I'm going to rise up against this coup."

"With whom?" Ned asked.

"With me, myself and I, and anyone else who's not afraid to be free in himself."

"Vladimir, you know all too well what happened at Tiananmen Square."

"Of course I do, the tanks ran over the people while the world watched."

"Then, you still have your wits about you. You're not going to do something drastic to get yourself killed are you?"

"Yes and no, in that yes I have my wits about me, and no I'm not going to do something drastic to get myself killed. Rather, I'm going to do something drastic to stop us from killing ourselves by hiding from our freedom to choose."

"Then what are you going to do?"

"I'm going to take my tank and stand with the people so that any tank who tries to run over them will first have to run over me in my T-72 tank. At Tiananmen, the world watched one man stand against a tank. Now, the world can watch one man in a tank stand against every other tank in the world, if necessary, and stand with the people."

"Vladimir, I'm afraid Raisa was right, even if for the wrong reason, for you don't stand a Holy Ghost of a chance!"

"Ned, you're forgetting again, you just called me the Holy Ghost," he replied, with an apparently irrational but most reasonable smile hinting to the fact that there's a reason beyond rationality.

"Isn't it ironic," Vladimir continued to speak in revealing superior reasoning," how the pendulum of life swings back and forth. You use to try to convert me to belief in your faith and now that I see the light, you're an unbeliever, you've lost your own faith."

"Vladimir, we're not talking about belief here now, you've got to face the facts."

"That's what I'm here for now, Ned, to face the facts, but the first fact before facing any others is that you've got to be more than a realist to face facts, more than a believer who believes in belief. You've got to see in order to believe, to have vision in order to see the potential for change, to know where to look inside before you can have insight, to visualize the right way before you can go the right way. I've seen it, Ned, I know the right way, and that's right to my T-72 and right to the barricades."

"So, Lieutenant Colonel Lubyanka issues an order, his order for himself, as a man, first, which will surely be countermanded by the coup in a second. You can't command your men as their commander, Lt. Colonel Lubyanka. But you can order yourself as Vladimir, as a personal command for others, at best some very few if any others, to follow. All right then, I'll just call you Vladimir, just like the old days at Albany. Since you intend to defend the barricades, however, I'll start with some facts and finish with some hard facts that you cannot ignore in carrying out your vision."

"Yeltsin spoke at 12:30 this afternoon to Katharina and a small group of supporters, numbering no more than a couple of hundred, urging the people to resist the coup. They're taking the construction building supplies and materials left around the Russian Parliament to erect more extensive barricades that they'll man and woman throughout the night. Their numbers are growing every minute and they'll soon be in the thousands. The news is being sent out from the Russian Parliament White House and broadcast with the assistance of the BBC, Voice of America and Radio Liberty. The *coupspirators* are going to call a press conference at 5:00 pm, but they won't be able to stop the people without using force."

"I've obtained the complete facts and inside knowledge about the coup plotters and the forces at their disposal. I'm afraid that the more I tell you, and I must tell you everything, the less you'll want to follow your vision."

"Tell me the facts, Ned."

CHAPTER ELEVEN

The Vosmyorka Gang of Eight

"First, the composition of the Vosmyorka, the Gang of Eight, the State Committee for the State of Emergency *coupspirators* is as follows: I've already mentioned their front man, Vice President Gennadi "S.S." Yanayev, the middle initials standing for sap and sob. The coup's *apparat* rat of a wimp attained the Vice Presidency only after a second round of voting in the Congress of People's Deputies, and that was accomplished only because of strong lobbying by Gorbachev. Any time there's pressure, Yanayev goes to pieces. Typically, his hands shake, his teeth rattle and his eyes roll - expect a lot of shake, rattle and roll from Gennadi."

"Then there's Valentine, 'the unloving Valentine Pavlov,' who as Prime Minister has been spending very unloving valentines highly critical of Gorbachev's policies. His porky countenance and *pavlovian* pout has gained him the apt nickname of 'Porky the Hedgehog.' He's highly unpopular and hyper, likely to live up to his nickname in being one of the first, along with shake rattle and roll Yanayev, to pig out in a *pavlovian* reaction under pressure. If the other six were like these two, there'd be little more to this *Moscoup* than a Moscow circus performance by a clown and a pig. Unfortunately, that's not the case."

"There's Vladimir 'krooked' Kryuchkov, who was appointed KGB chairman by Gorbachev in 1988, a man of all crooked maneuvers and no substance, a go with the criminal flow personality."

"Next there's Dimitri 'yes sir, no sir' Yazov, a stone-faced old World War II veteran who was reappointed Defense Minister in 1989 due to Gorbachev's backing. He's a yea sayer to perestroika and a nay sayer to glasnost. He's in it because he's strongly opposed to glasnost as a means with which others, especially Yeltsin, have criticized abuses in the military.

"The next man is Oleg 'one leg up' Baklanov, who's got one leg up on the rest as the influential First Deputy on the Soviet Defense Council. He's a very important member of the military - industrial

69

complex whose edifice complex , 25% of the Gross National Product, has been exposed as the 'Gross' national neurosis that it is."

"Every group has their Judas, and Valeri 'the' bold Boldin more than qualifies for his designation as Gorbachev's Judas of the *coupspiracy*. He took a really bold step in stabbing Gorbachev in the back; he was his chief of staff and a personal aide since 1981 when he was brought into the political inner circle by Gorbachev, himself. Boldin was the last person anyone would have suspected."

"Next there's 'Lucky' Anatoli 'cool hand Luk' Lukyanov. Cool hand Luk was an old school buddy and close friend of Gorbachev, who recently assumed his lucky ways in receiving the designation as his likely successor. As Chairman of the Supreme Soviet, he played his lucky hand in cooling off liberals by turning off the microphones of liberal deputies to prevent them from being heard. I also discovered that in the early hours of the coup, he tried to cool the democratic opposition by spreading rumors that Gorbachev approved of the takeover in luckily leaving Moscow so that the *Moscoupers* could get on with their business. In this respect, I believe that cool hand Luk and Boris Pugo were the respective brains and brawn behind this less than respectful State Committee."

"Last and worst, there's Boris 'the Pugolist' Pugo, nicknamed by me for his pugilistic inclination in fighting reform. He's a top cop with a *throughred* Party pedigree, who was appointed Interior Minister last year in response to right wing complaints that a liberal reform Interior Ministry had resulted in public disorder. There's strong suspicion, even for those without suspicious minds, that he was the behind the scenes instigator who provoked violence in the Baltics as a pretext for a violent crackdown by Omon's black berets. He'll let all hell loose in cracking down on the demonstrators. It's him or them, the Pugolist or the democrats, who'll be down for the final countdown."

"In reference to the deployment of forces, the Vitebskaya, the airborne KGB division I told you about this morning is already on the move less than twenty miles from Moscow. In addition, the KGB has 230,000 border troops who are currently stretched out along the entire length of the Soviet Union's borders. They can be brought in as well but it will take some time to do so."

"The Kantemirovskaya Armored division along with the Tulskaya Airborne Division are already in Moscow. The Alpha Group is also in Moscow, specially trained and equipped to storm buildings like the Russian Parliament just as the buildings held by the Lithuanian demonstrators in Vilnius were taken last January. The difference now being that there are many more thousands of demonstrators in Moscow leading to the prospect of many more thousands of casualties."

"Pugo as Interior Minister has 300,000 Internal Troops, controlled by the MVD, the Internal Ministry at his command. Add to them the Omon, the black omen to the Baltics, the black berets, the Special Mission Militia, organized in 35 crack units, with an inside estimate of their total strength at 30,000, who also fall under the control of the MVD."

"In addition to the Vitebskaya and the border troops, the KGB also his 40,000 special purpose troops, the Spetsznas forces as they're known. What you may not know, however, is how they train their men. What they do is train them in one on one fights to the death with convicted murderers sentenced to death who can obtain their release from prison if they survive by killing their Spetsznas opponent. A somewhat risky way of qualifying for a parole reprieve from capital punishment, you might say."

"Expect all of the above to be coming against you, Vladimir, not to mention the 1,473,000 regular army troops backed up by two million more men in the air force and navy. In case you may have lost count, you're facing approximately four million men who are under orders to reestablish law and order. When you take your stand, in your tank, you'll be the one clear military target that all of them can zero in on, in targeting you as one total zero.

"Graphically put, Ned, and as usual you're more than done your homework in getting all the facts and information I requested. I really appreciate knowing everything and if you get more information, please bring it to me where you can reach me at the barricades."

"Were you listening to me?" Ned responded with growing frustration, "I said four million men, four million to one, that's your chance my friend!"

"It's good to know the odds," Vladimir replied still smiling with calm assurance, "when you choose to gamble."

"You're gambling with your life at odds of four million to one against you, and you still expect me to consider you sane!"

"I remember part of the lyrics to an old American love song, something like 'a million to one . . . .' it's just that my lyrics are multiplied to 4 million to one. You've forgotten something again, Ned. Tell me, aren't Katharina's odds even less for she's there right now, and she'll stay there to the end with no weapon and no protection except the shield of her spirit. I won't leave her alone for my T-72 is her protection and the sword of my spirit."

"She's in a different situation, she's use to democratic demonstrations."

"No, Ned, on that one point you're dead wrong. When you face death it's the same, not different. Further, in answer to your question about my sanity, I'm both quite sane and wonderfully insane. I'm sane by American standards because I know exactly what the facts of the situation are, thanks to you, and I know what's right and wrong. I know it's wrong to follow any other order than one's own personal order for freedom. As to freedom, my freedom, her freedom and others freedom, I'm making my own order above any other. So, in that respect, I'm sane but, also, you're right in one respect in that in one way I'm not sane. Rather, I'm wonderfully insane in being beyond sanity in the insanity of love, without which life and freedom are truly insane."

"I like the odds, Ned, for if I lose, the odds rather than what I'm fighting for will have lost; but if I win, I win for those four million as well as the six billion people in the world. You might say if I lose, it was a four million to one gamble; but if I win, it's a one to six billion success – more than a thousand times greater success than if I lose. If those forces that you've reported to me attack, I'll be killed; but what I'll have done will go on living like the Chinese student in front of the tank - as an illustration of the reality of freedom and as an example to inspire others just as Christians are inspired by the death of Jesus."

"I'm sane enough to know fully well what I'm going to do for freedom," Vladimir concluded his explanation with the sanest of explanations, "and insane enough in love to freely do it."

"Yes, my good Christian friend, in response to your concern about my sanity, I'm just as sane and insane as was Jesus!"

CHAPTER TWELVE

Vladimir: Unknown Soldier and Patron Saint of Everyone's Unknown Fight for Freedom

"Whether you live or die in doing what you're about to do," Ned replied in a subdued tone of awe and reverence, "you'll be commemorated by your call to Just Call Me Vladimir. You'll be known as more than the unknown soldier, and more as the unknown saint called Vladimir for everyone's unknown fight for freedom."

"Vladimir, Christians debate among themselves whether it's better to save oneself according to a personal gospel or serve the world according to a social gospel. You've shown me that the debate is unnecessary for one can only save oneself by doing what he can - sane and insane - to serve the world. Those Christians who quote Jesus in support of laying down ones life (almost invariably someone else's life) for another would better see Jesus differently in picking up one's life for others."

JESUIT (ORDER OF CATHOLIC PRISTS)

"When we were students together so many years ago, I use to like debating with you in using my Jesuitical training to win on points. Today, you've won in pointing out to me what's right about love and freedom. You've won every point this time, Vladimir, because you can see everything."

"As you leave to go to your men, I correct myself in stating that I no longer see a man who's going to his death, but a man who's facing death in order to live. You haven't, I can clearly see now, died to yourself in order to live. Rather you're dead to an old self and alive to your new self in order to love as the only way to live for yourself. I've learned from you what I thought I knew better by seeing what you see better. One can never lay down one's life for another, only pick it up to love another."

"I'll see you at the barricades, it's now four million to two, four million to the two of us," Ned spoke with his head out the window as Vladimir turned back to his car and ,then, stood at the door to turn and wave goodbye to him before getting back into his car.

"Ned", Vladimir yelled, "you forgot something again, it's four million to three, you forgot Katharina!"

"Four million to three it is, the odds are getting better every second," Ned yelled back, as they drove off in separate but equal directions. Ned drove off to meet Katharina at the barricades, while Vladimir sped off in the opposite direction to meet his men at their T-72 tanks.

As he drove through the main gate to his office in the staff headquarters of his division, Vladimir recounted the legacy of his military unit, the one division in the immense Soviet land armada about which he knew every detail without any need of Ned's intelligence gathering skills.

CHAPTER THIRTEEN

The Tamanskaya Guards Guarding the Kremlin From Democratic Gremlins

The Tamanskaya Guards Division was founded in 1940 as the 127th Infantry Division, receiving their Guards honor title in 1941, when they were renamed as the 2nd Guards Infantry Division. In World War II this highly decorated unit suffered over 10,000 casualties and earned 33 Hero of the Soviet Union awards and approximately 19,000 other military awards and medals. Vladimir's father, a private in this unit during the Great War, died in battle to live on as one of those 33 Heroes of the Soviet Union.

The officer corps, consisting of 4,000 professional soldiers like him, oversaw conscripts from all 15 republics representing 53 nationalities. This elite division was one of the few that did not see service in Afghanistan, being kept close to home for the more important task of securing the Kremlin from democratic gremlins. The Field Commander, Full Colonel Valeri Marchenkov, had been summoned to Moscow earlier that day to receive his orders and had not yet returned. Taking advantage of his temporary absence, Vladimir summoned the Colonel's assistant, Major Alexander Chistiyakov, to his office.

Major Chistiyakov immediately reported in standing at attention before his desk and saluting, "Major Chistiyakov reporting for duty as ordered, Sir."

"Major," Vladimir addressed him, while he stood at attention without allowing him the customary military headquarters courtesy to a major grade officer of standing at ease, "I've issued a parade dress call to speak to the men in five minutes and I'm taking full responsibility for whatever happens. Accordingly, I'm assigning you to your desk for the rest of the day with orders to see and speak with no one from outside."

"Sir," the major replied in stunned disbelief, "if Colonel Marchenkov or one of his general superiors call, Ill have to speak with them, won't I?"

"The answer is No!" Vladimir responded, with the sternest command tone and military countenance, "you're not to see or speak with anyone or answer your phone anytime today, that's a direct order, is that clear?"

"Yes, sir, it's clear."

Major Chistiyakov had risen, like himself, quickly through the ranks in distinguishing himself by never modifying let alone disobeying an order. He was confident he'd do what he was told; and since Colonel Marchenkov had not yet returned with his orders, the way to his men and the gate to Moscow were wide open.

"Major, sit down." I'd like to talk with you not as Lieutenant Colonel Lubyanka, but as a man who's known you for a long time. Here, have a cigarette."

"Thanks sir," he hesitantly replied as he awkwardly took the cigarette and sat down.

"I want to speak to you as a man, first, and as an officer, second."

"Yes sir," the major responded in an anxious quip, while exhibiting a nervous twitch that made it difficult for him to light his cigarette.

"Alexander, my friend, relax and Just Call Me Vladimir, not Sir," he stated, in reminding himself of his encounter years before with President Vincent Sullivan, who refused to be addressed as Sir. In this situation, however, he was acting like Sullivan and the major was now feeling what Vladimir felt then.

"May I ask you, Vladimir, what you intend to do?"

"Yes, you most certainly may, and I'll be glad to tell you. I'm going to speak with the men as men, first, and soldiers, second," he replied, as he stood up to take a folder from the file cabinet and returned to his desk.

"Alexander, please listen carefully to what I'm going to read to you:

> 'We strongly hope a lasting peace will come and as professional soldiers we are happy to participate in and we support the new cause of direction. You must remember the army is part of Soviet society and not apart from it.' "

"Do you recall the statement?" Vladimir asked, as he looked up directly at him.

"Yes, it was what I wrote two years ago for a visiting British reporter to publish in Jane's Defense Weekly."

"You and Colonel Marchenkov are both members of Shield, The Union for the Social Protection of Servicemen and Reservists are you not?"

"Yes, Vladimir, we are."

"Also, some of the men in our unit have been involved with Shield as a grass roots military reform organization to bring reform to generals along with reform for civilians in general, correct?"

"I can see in the file that Shield hosted a congress for 176 delegates in Moscow on December 15th and 16th, 1991, whereat Yeltsin was the guest speaker."

"Yes, and I was there with Colonel Manchenkov."

"And how many of our tankers were there as well?"

"I'd say between thirty to forty."

"Then, you've already answered much of your own question about what I intend to do. I'm going to speak to those men to volunteer to go with me and live up to those very words that you've written for the international press."

"How many T-72s are fully combat ready at this minute?"

"Ten in addition to your own, Sir...excuse me, Vladimir," the Major quickly corrected his lapse back into military address in responding to a military assessment.

"Then, Alexander, when I leave with one tank, my tank, or with ten more tanks, you know what I'm doing and where I'm going and why! I'm going to defend the Russian White House and the man you've been listening to and writing about for two years."

"But, Vladimir, what can I do if they order me to stop you?"

"You can refuse the order."

"I've never refused an order in my life."

"Neither have I before today, but today is the first day that I know I can order my own life."

"Do you expect me to do what you're going to do?"

"I don't expect anything of you except to follow my order for the day not to accept any other order today."

"They should be assembled now," Vladimir quickly glanced at this watch, as he rose to leave his office.

"Alexander, think about what you said in your writings two years ago, and do what you can do to help us. I can't and won't try to order you to join us - how many or few of us there'll be - but at least for today, for the few remaining hours left in this day, can I count on you not coming against us?"

He stood there with his eyes to the ground, a man not easily given to a new order and commitment that questioned the order of his life. Slowly, but without hesitation, he looked up at Vladimir and spoke, "It's a standing order that all combat ready T-72 tanks should be given quick and ready access. Be quick, Vladimir, and I'll be ready to give you the access to quickly get out of here with your T-72s."

They both smiled as they walked down the corridor together, smiling at something new in themselves that made them free in themselves. They reached the front door of the Tamanskaya Guards headquarters facing the assembled tankers at parade formation. As Vladimir shook his hand, Alexander suddenly embraced him and then just as suddenly pulled back to state, "Something just went wrong with out communication and telephone lines, they don't seem to work today."

"That's what happens when you don't have AT&T," Vladimir smiled, as he headed towards the division parade ground.

In walking across the parade ground he observed the three man tank crews standing at parade rest in unit formation with First Lieutenants in the right column each with a sergeant and a corporal lined up next to them. Arriving closer to them, he felt neither fear nor courage, hesitation nor exhilaration, only the overwhelming necessity to forget himself. He would give his last speech to them which might be his last speech to anyone. He'd do so not as their commanding officer with an order for the day, but as a man whose identity had blended into and become one with the vision that would free them to command themselves and order their lives for the rest of their days. For twenty years he'd unfreely given and taken orders without thinking about what was true or false; but, today, he'd give no order nor quarter in taking his freedom to speak the truth.

The truth, he knew, hurts, in thinking of his earlier moment of truth with Raisa, but it sets one free. It can be both cruel and liberating, kind and brutal, a salvation or a damnation. This dual aspect of truth can be explained by one's reaction to it. If one chooses to lie to oneself, to believe what's contrary to what's true, truth hurts; if one chooses to choose for oneself rather than be chosen by others, truth frees. Having chosen to make the choice for freedom, thereby making himself a chosen person in the only legitimate way one can be chosen, he stepped up to the military field podium and looked out at the assembled tank crews before him as if he were speaking to a new chosen people.

"Men of the T-72 tank units of the Tamanskaya Guards, I've called you here, today, to speak with you for the first time in our many years together as someone other than Lieutenant Colonel Lubyanka. You all know that there was a coup this morning and opposition has already begun with civilians constructing barricades to defend the Russian Parliament. I've called you here to speak with you in a way that I've never spoken to anyone before - even to myself."

"No longer can I order you, nor do I want to address you, as your Lieutenant Colonel, for the time for an old order is gone and the time for a new order is now. I speak with you as just Vladimir, a free man, first, and a military man, second; and I speak to all of you as free men from every republic and nationality in the Soviet Union."

"During our Fatherland's Patriotic War, my father served and died in this unit; and I was sent to the military academy as a boy to continue his legacy as a Hero of the Soviet Union. Many of you close to my age also grew up without your fathers, approximately twenty million, who died fighting against the Nazi hordes. When our country's back was against the Kremlin's wall and the blood of our fathers was flowing like a flood throughout our lands, Stalin changed his mind about the ancient beliefs of this land. He temporarily allowed religious worship to reappear, and icons to be seen, and saints to be prayed to, and Bibles and Korans to be quoted. He allowed it not because he wanted to but because he didn't want to lose the war. This Communist so called opiate of the people, the Mass of the masses, the religion of the people became a miraculous super drug, a national infusion called upon by believer and unbeliever, alike, so that our country could be saved from national socialism and, as a result, save the world."

"Our fathers took the brunt of that world struggle with the result that so many millions of us were left without fathers. While over thirty countries fought the Nazis, we were the one country that defeated them. At no time in our war for survival did we ever face less than two thirds of the might of the Hitlerites. Our country, our families and most of all we, as Tamanskaya Guards, have much to be proud of in our military heritage that all of us share. However, although our fathers wiped out the foreign disease of national socialism, we, as their sons, fell ill to an internal disease that became the world epidemic of international socialism."

"Some of our Soviet forces - not us - but others have openly and with impunity killed democratic demonstrators in Latvia and Lithuania while the KGB has quietly killed many others in every other republic. Boris Yeltsin has spoken to some of you, those of you who are members of Shield, about putting a stop to those deaths and any others. Now, his back is against the wall of the Russian White House, and the blood of our civilian friends on the barricades of democracy is about to flow once more in a river of blood through this land. The decision you make, each of you as a free man, is just as momentous for our country and the world as the decision our fathers made. An invader is here once again with an internal terminal disease of their law and order with the deadly symptoms of their denial of our freedom. If we fall sick to this illness, there will be a Black plague epidemic of Black berets all over this country and a return to a cold war and ,perhaps, even hot and cold wars all over the world."

CHAPTER FOURTEEN

Icon of Mother Russia as Ican to a Promised Land of the Promise of Freedom

"We are, you and me and each one of us, on the verge of entering into our own promised land of freedom or forever wandering in the desert of communism. I can see and I hope you, too, will see with me a promised land of personal freedom and political democracy. The land I see doesn't promise milk and honey, rather it holds the promise of being whatever we're free enough to make it. When I take my T-72 tank to enter into our Russian promised land, I do so not to slay the communist inhabitants thereof, including soldiers deployed against me, but to save them. I not only believe and know, but I can see that our promised land is, indeed, a land promised by God to us, for God's promised land is any land with the promise of God's freedom. Any other promise based on slaying is slavery, a slaying of others in slavery to oneself."

"As I look out at you I see faces I've served with for many years, and I see men who represent the various beliefs of our peoples that Stalin prayed to in his atheistic prayer for our land's salvation. I see Russian Orthodox, Catholics, Lutherans, Pentecostals, Muslims and Jews; and I want to speak with each of you the best way I can according to your beliefs.

To the majority Russian Orthodox like myself, I hold up to you our ancient icons of Mother Russia and I ask you to make a choice. I call upon you to choose the Russian Icon as your personal Ican, seeing to it that the Ican becomes your personal Ican to freedom. Those of you in the enlisted ranks are mostly conscripts, chosen by others while the officers among you chose to become part of the Guards. Now, I ask you to use the common Ican of your common mother, Russia, to come together in common prayer under her Icon as your common Ican vision and example of democracy for every nationality represented in our unit and in our Union. Those of you who've been chosen must choose, along with those who've already chose to become chosen together, in the only way the chosen can be God's chosen - by choosing freedom for all."

"To the Catholics among you, most of whom are Ukrainian and Lithuanian, I personally apologize to you and ask your forgiveness for what your people and lands have suffered at the hands of Soviet Communists, many of whom were Russian. You believe in and pray to saints as men and women who showed what God was so that others might see what they might be. Today is your Holy Day of Obligation, a day obligated by your choice to be holy in taking freedom from a holistic concept to a wholly Real Presence. This is your day to become a saint for both saints and sinners in showing the way to what might be. Many of your Catholic saints died as martyrs, but they died in a way that showed the power of everlasting life over any death. I'm not asking you to lay down your life for me or any others, but to pick it up in your T-72s for yourselves and others."

"To the Pentecostals among you, let me say that the Baptism of fire of the Holy Spirit is upon us, in the spiritual fire of freedom calling us to rise up in the name of that which comes to us from above. Let me quote your favorite passage from Scripture: Acts 2:17 as our passage together:

> 'And it shall come to pass in the last days, said God, I will pour out of my Spirit upon all flesh: and your sons and your daughters shall prophesy, and your young men shall see visions, and your old men shall dream dreams.'"

"My friends in the Spirit, the Spirit of freedom which is part of the Spirit of God is now pouring out upon the flesh of those sons and daughters, who prophesize on the barricades of freedom. Our parents could only dream of the vision we see before us. It's now your last day to let God's vision indwell in your spirit in a new Pentecost of freedom."

"To the followers of Martin Luther, the great reformer and fighter for Christian freedom, I say that Martin Luther would be with us today if he were alive. Like Luther, who fought personal demons and transformed the demons of his time, we have to fight our demons and transform those who intermediate political democracy with their communist *demonocracy*."

"Luther could see his way out because of his vision of salvation by faith alone. If he taught us anything it is this: that you are responsible directly to God for your own freedom. We know from the Bible that even with faith, a faith without works is dead; and I know that while you can't work your way to faith, if you have faith you must work it out with faithful vision. Luther's Amen was a BE IT SO vision to a religious future with freedom in a reformation away from a So Be It Amen to the religious dictates of the past."

"Once again, my Lutheran friends, the way out for you and all of us is our common prayer Amen to a past dictatorial So Be It, in making our Amen of a free BE IT So vision our future!"

"To my brothers from Azerbaijan, Kazakhstan, Kyrgyzstan, Tajikistan, Turkmenia and Uzbekistan, I speak to you in the name of one God and your Allah with a quote from the Koran. "No soul,' it states, 'can ever die except by Allah's leave and at a time appointed.'"

"The appointed time is now my brothers, for now is the point in time for you to choose in your own way, in your own decision for life and death, what Allah asks of you. Listen not to what I say, but to what your soul says, in making your eternal appointment with Him. Better to arrive for your appointment on time than too late."

"Last, to the few Jews among you, I have perhaps the most to say or, at least, the most important things to say. Your religion for those of you who are religious, and your history for those of you who are not, is one that records for all of us the words of your prophets warning your people about the dangers of turning away from God. You, as a people, have suffered terrible judgments, the most terrible being the Nazi holocaust, from which we as a nation also suffered terribly."

"Today, you along with the rest of us have to make a judgment, which in many ways is also a terrible judgment, for we must together face the cruelty of an ideological holocaust that destroys any and all other ideological identities. I believe that your God and our God is a just God but that justice demands what is just for all of us. There is, as stated in your psalms, a time to forgive and a time to fight. Now is the time to fight and tomorrow will be time enough to forgive. As with my Muslim brothers, I also consider you to be my Jewish brothers and, accordingly, I'd like to quote to you from your Talmud. It states that 'To show mercy to the cruel is to show cruelty to the innocent.' The innocents are waiting in the barricades and not to act, now, in their defense are to condone the cruelty of a Pharaoh's slaughter."

"I'd like to conclude my special appeal to you and to all of us with a reference to a very special tradition that you, as Jews, have in reference to the survival of the world. According to Jewish tradition, the universe and our world in it survives because of thirty six righteous men, the Lamed-Overnice, whose identities are hidden so that the world does not know about them. I will need all thirty six of them today."

"I had no idea this morning that I'd be here this afternoon to speak with you or that I'd be speaking to all of you in this way. A few hours ago, I took off my insignia bearing the rank of Lieutenant Colonel and asked people who've known me all their lives as a career professional soldier and officer to Just Call Me Vladimir."

As he spoke, he thought of Raisa and Ned along with Vera, his mother and Katharina, his lover, the two women who'd always called him just Vladimir.

"I ask all of you now to do the same, to make your choice with me, as just Vladimir, for no longer am I your Commanding Officer, Lieutenant Colonel Lubyanka. I'm freely in command of myself, and I hereby release you from my command in order to free each of you to make the choice of taking command of yourself. Those of you, if there are any of you who choose to go with me, who follow, will follow me according to your own order to yourself rather than any order from me. There are ten fully equipped combat ready T-72 tanks waiting for ten tank crews, for thirty more righteous men to join me.

As he spoke, Vladimir realized that there were already some righteous people, some of whom the Orthodox might not totally approve, but whom God and the feminists certainly would in that two of them were women. His mother, Vera, was the first righteous women for being right in her vision, and Katharina, his lover, was the second for being right about love. Ned was the third in having the right information and still choosing to help him in face of the odds, and the Major was the fourth in doing the right thing at the right moment in providing quick access to the tanks.

"You men will be, like me, just called Vladimir, known only to me and unknown to the rest of the world. There will be no last names or identities revealed in order to protect you and your families whom the coup may attempt to punish in retaliation. Together, we will all be unknown Vladimirs, unknown righteous men who freely choose more than a new world order in choosing our personal order for our new world of freedom."

As he stepped down from the podium and walked to the tanks, he realized that if his tankers followed him, there would be thirty three righteous men. Ned and the Major would make thirty five righteous men. Nevertheless, he'd still be one short in missing one more righteous man. That thirty sixth righteous man would be needed to save all of them and, accordingly, save the world in the process. That was what the Jewish prophecy said, and even though he wasn't a Jewish believer he believed the Jewish prophecy.

CHAPTER FIFTEEN

Russian Colors

Arriving at the tank assembly area behind the parade grounds, he saw eleven T-72 tanks in their sheds with the restraining gates unlocked. Major Chistiyakov had, as he'd promised, quickly unlocked the tank sheds and was already opening the main front gate, while directing the placement of road signals indicating an impending tank formation exit from the base. Vladimir walked over to the first tank, which was his personal lead tank, and tore off the small hammer and sickle Soviet display flag replacing it with a huge white, blue and red Russian tricolor. The Major had more than completed their preparation in providing eleven Russian flags which were left neatly folded and placed on top of each tank's gun turret.

Just as he finished striking the Russian colors on his tank, he saw First Lieutenant Israel Horowitz, along with his own tank crew mingling with Horowitz's tank crew.

"Vladimir, let me introduce myself as Vladimir, your first unknown righteous man accompanied by two Sergeant Vladimirs and two Corporal Vladimirs at your call," Lieutenant Horowitz introduced himself, and the combined tank crews, without the customary salute.

"That you are, Israel . . .," Vladimir hesitated and corrected himself, "I mean Vladimir," overjoyed in the coincidence of the first Lamed - Vovenic being a Jew."

"Are there any others?" Vladimir asked him as he looked around.

"I don't know," Horowitz responded.

"Well, then, it's your tank and mine. Take your tank and follow me out to the gate."

"Right away, sir . . . I mean Vladimir," Lieutenant Horowitz replied, as they both adjusted themselves to a new command structure of a voluntary ordering of themselves in contrast to their years of being ordered to order.

The roar of the two tanks blocked out any other sound, as they road to the front gate in top gear leaving a blinding cloud of dust behind them. In a deafening roar and a blinding cloud of dust, dirt and smoke they approached the front gate to exit out onto the road to Moscow.

"Stop!" Major Chistiyakov yelled and gestured, as he ran out in front to stop their exit.

"Stop Vladimir!"

Vladimir brought his tank to a jolting halt with Lieutenant Horowitz doing the same less than fifteen yards behind him. They could barely see each other or the Major through the further clouds of dust raised by their abrupt stop.

"What's wrong, Alexander?"

"There's only one thing wrong, Vladimir, and that is you're going too fast."

"I'm sorry Major, but I may have to break some speed limits today."

"It's not the speed limit that's the problem," the Major yelled, with his voice barely discernable above the noise of the engines, and his person being all but invisible in the clouds of dust.

"What is it then?"

"Turn around, Vladimir, and look. You've got more tanks trying to catch up to you."

He turned to see nine T-72s in column formation all striking the tricolors as he waited for them to catch up.

"Major, if in your official capacity you receive any inquiries as to who's manning these tanks just tell them Vladimir," he yelled to the Major, whom he could finally see again in the receding clouds of dust, as he signaled all of the T-72s forward to their destination and their destiny.

"Vladimir," the Major yelled back, as the tanks prepared to turn onto the road for their twenty five mile drive to the Russian White House, "if they ask me who gave the command, I'll tell them that Vladimir, whomever he is, gave it to another unknown Vladimir, who gave it to another."

"That's right, Major, and tell them to expect at least one more Vladimir," he replied, in the absolute confidence that there would be another righteous man, a thirty sixth Vladimir, to fulfill both the Jewish prophecy and his mother's Christian vision.

They arrived at the Russian Parliament later that evening having taken every precaution to avoid any entanglement or confrontation with other military units in their path. They approached the barricades at 11:40 pm. as Vladimir commanded the tanks to stop, in realizing that the demonstrators might not be able to see the Russian tricolors in the darkness. He jumped on top of his tank and waived the Russian tricolors so that the nervous demonstrators behind the barricades would know that they were friends and not foes.

"Katharina, Katharina, are you there?" he screamed out, at the top of his lungs, to the democratic defenders, who were fearfully peering out at him and his tank from behind their makeshift barricades. "I'm over here, Vladimir," a voice from the front left of the barricades responded, as she calmed the others in assuring them that the tanks had come to defend them rather than attack them.

Immediately, Katharina and the rest of the demonstrators started to tear down a section of their hastily constructed barricade to allow the tanks to enter. Minutes later, Vladimir and his eleven T-72 tanks were inside with their guns facing out and away from the Russian White House so as to defend it rather than attack it. The message was soon to be made clear to those on both sides of the barricades that the stakes had changed. The military odds against those behind the barricades were still overwhelming; but, now, the military was at odds with itself in having to face its most elite tank unit. The message was that some unknown tank commander, in positioning his tanks to defend rather than attack freedom, had changed the moral odds. That unknown tank commander would soon be referred to by those on both sides of the barricades as just Vladimir.

"Katharina," he smiled, as he climbed down from his tank to embrace her, "I promised you this morning that I'd see you later, today, or else you'd never see me again."

She looked down at her watch and replied, "It's exactly 11:59 pm. You kept your promise with only a minute to spare," she whispered, as she leaned forward to kiss and embrace him in their leaning against his tank.

"Vladimir, my love, you've made everything different for us, our country, even our world by coming here."

"My dear Katharina, you made me different by first coming to me, and, then, coming here. You made me see the truth of a vision."

"What might they do to you now?" she started to cry.

"All they can do," he answered her, by holding her tearful face in his hands as he tenderly looked at her and smiled, "is to try to find out who I am, for all of us here are just like me in being just Vladimir!"

She attempted to smile back at him in half smiling and half crying, as they began to laugh at her tears.

"I'll tell everyone when the reporters come and inquire to call you and all your men, Vladimir!"

"Vladimir It Is… for all of us tankers. That's my name and that's our name in this game of life and death that I can win only with your love."

"You have my love, darling, and you always will. You may be an unknown Vladimir to the world, but to me you're the Vladimir I know who has made my world."

"The odds keep getting better, don't they," a voice spoke out in the darkness, as Ned stepped out from the crowd assembled around the tanks to embrace both of them.

"What's our situation Ned?" Vladimir responded as they embraced, in asking for a military briefing as to the likelihood and timing of an attack.

"They won't attack tonight when they see your tanks. They'll need time to change to new weaponry."

"You must be referring to the Alpha Group, Ned, for we know the weaponry of the conventional forces."

"Yes, I am referring to them, let's talk alone," Ned spoke, as he walked with him away from the barricade defenders and the tanks to a spot where they could speak without being overhead.

"The Alpha Group commander has been ordered to prepare an attack plan for taking the Russian Parliament based on tactics similar to those used against the demonstrators defending the communications building in Vilnius, Lithuania. The attack was expected to occur early Tuesday morning right before dawn. Now, however, with your tanks defending these people and the White House, they'll have to use a new weapon that's been developed with the highest secrecy and never used before in combat, not even in Afghanistan."

"Why hasn't it been used before?"

"It hasn't been used for the reason that the military didn't want the West to know about this new technology. They've been saving this weapon for a life or death defense of the Kremlin rather than letting intelligence get out about it by using it in Afghanistan."

"What am I facing?"

"You're facing a new rocket launched neutron missile, a weapon that has the characteristics of a neutron bomb but one that can be fired with pinpoint accuracy from a modified shoulder fired rocket launcher."

"Its delivery system sounds similar to the nuclear artillery shells developed for the Atomic Canon at Fort Sill, Oklahoma, by your American artillery specialists."

"Yes, the analogy is correct in that both of these armor and artillery weapon systems developed theater area nuclear technology for platoon and even squad level application. Furthermore, Vladimir, this new weapons system is the one system with which, this time, Soviet specialists have surpassed those in the West."

"Do you know the target area impact effects of this new weapon?"

"No one knows exactly since it hasn't been tested on people, yet, but I do know that it destroys all life in its range while leaving equipment and buildings undamaged. I've also learned that it has a special laser component that somehow scrambles and destroys human brain cells. You are facing, literally, a mind destroying weapon!

"What is its armor piercing capacity?"

"I'm not sure for I don't know how much armor piercing it has. But I'd surmise that if it were not able to penetrate your T-72 armor, they would first use armor piercing shells against your tanks and then hit you with it on the second shot."

"So then, they might need two direct hits to terminate us."

"Yes, I'd say there's a chance that they may need two hits."

"Then if we can stop them before or even immediately after their first attack, we might be safe."

"If incredible good luck is on your side, yes, for a while, a short while, but you'll have to be very sure, at that, to avoid a lethal armor piercing first strike."

"What do you think as a former artillery officer our chances are?"

"Vladimir, I don't think you have much of a chance at all. You have next to no mobility, no cover and hardly any fire direction control from your side. Basically, you'll be sitting in your tank like a sitting duck in a tank pond. And while you can make them pay a price in blood, there's no doubt that, sooner or later, you and your men will be dead ducks."

"Ned, there's one quality about you that I've always admired but, frankly, one that I wish you didn't have at this moment. That's your total inability to be evasive when the reality of the situation is so damn awful."

"I'm not going to lie to you now, my friend, and I don't think you should hide the truth from your men either."

"I've never lied to my men before and I don't want to lie to them now, either, but if I tell them the truth and they decide to leave, Katharina, you and everyone else here on these barricades will be shooting ducks."

CHAPTER SIXTEEN

Blessing of Being Chosen and Curse of Being Chosin

"Vladimir, tell them the truth and tell them tonight while they still have time to choose. Katharina and you and me and these young people on the barricades are here because we've all chosen. Give your men the chance to make the final choice for themselves. Everyone has to choose how to face death in order to live. If they can't choose for themselves, instead of having the blessing of being chosen in having chosen, they'll have the curse of being *chosin*. That curse is the plight of any *chosin* person or people deluded by their sin of presuming to be what they can only make themselves to be by choice.

"Ned, as usual you're analytically and morally correct, I just feel that . . . well I don't know how to say it, but I feel that another unknown person is going to complete our mission for us."

"Maybe you're right, Vladimir; and you just may find more than I can by finding the answer in your vision."

"I'm going to spend the rest of the night talking to my tank commanders, all ten of them, in order to let them and each of their tank crews choose for themselves. In the meantime, keep an eye out for Katharina, will you. I'd like to know that while she's looking out for everyone else, someone's looking out for her."

"Don't worry, Vladimir, I will," Ned assured him, as they returned to their respective tasks of looking out for others.

Although Israel Horowitz was the first man to volunteer to go with him, he decided to speak with him last. Although he didn't know Horowitz that well, he knew that no matter what the threat, Horowitz would stand with him to the end. The rest of the tank leaders he knew by name only, in that most of them were First Lieutenants recently commissioned within the last two years. The officers he'd spent most of his ten years in the Guards serving with had been promoted to the ranks of captain and major in staff headquarters assignments. It was a typical example of the bureaucratic Peter Principle in the military

ask me about this 95 *I — unless you know*

practice of taking seasoned field commanders and promoting them to staff positions where their skills became mere seasoning to their unit's mission. In facing up to the greatest test that any officer or man could ever face, he's first have to face his untested junior grade officers before he could face down the Soviet military. More important than the military skills of his tank commanders in the face of the State Committee for the State of the Emergency, however, was the state of their minds which he intended to confront - face to face - in giving each of them a choice.

CHAPTER SEVENTEEN

The Tank Commanders

Accordingly, he went up to the closest tank, the last one to arrive inside the barricades to speak with its commander, First Lieutenant Yuri Mosyr and climbed inside his tank.

"Yuri, I need to brief you on our situation and let you choose to remain or leave. I've been informed that there's a strong likelihood of an Alpha Group attack with a special weapon. They have a recently developed rocket launched missile with devastating capabilities. If they use it against us, which they've been ordered to do, we'll be destroyed. They won't be able to deploy it until morning, and then it could happen any time. If you decide to leave, I understand, and if you do so, you should leave before dawn."

"Vladimir, I'll speak with my crew about their choice to stay or leave, but I've already made my choice to stay."

"Yuri, I know why I'm here, I'd like to know why you're here."

"I'm here because I'm Belorussian, but I'm not here to fight the old Belorussian, anti-Bolshevik fight against the Reds that many of our White Russian forebears fought. Rather, I'm here to fight a new battle, an even more crucial and universal fight for the future. My reason for choosing to be here, and to stay here, has nothing to do with any struggle between East and West; but it has everything to do with a human struggle in both East and West."

"What struggle is that?"

"It's a fight to save our children from environmental death that comes to them in the name of technology. You're aware, of course, of the Chernobyl nuclear accident, but only a few people are aware that this nuclear death is still being waged against us in a silent but incredibly deadly war."

"I thought that since 1985 with glasnost we've been able to finally deal with this problem and control it," Vladimir replied.

"That's what they'd like you to believe and, by them, I don't mean just the Soviet government."

"Who, then, are you referring to?"

"I'm telling you that with detente and glasnost and perestroika, all nice sounding words for East - West dialogue, the nuclear and chemical industries including the pharmaceutical - more accurately described as *harmaceutical*- have orchestrated an East-West symphony of silence and phony science in covering up their crimes against humanity."

"Prior to 1985 and Gorbachev, a nuclear meltdown of the kind that occurred at Three Mile Island near Harrisburg in the Commonwealth of Pennsylvania in the States was pointed to by the Communists as an example of capitalist exploitation of the people and the environment in the name of profits. Similarly, cases of environmental poisoning in Eastern Europe and the Soviet Union were eagerly sought out and publicized in the West as examples of Communist exploitation of the workers in whose behalf they claimed to govern. Now, this so called glasnost open door and perestroika new structure is used as a detente mechanism whereby these environmental killers - and that's what their pollution does - can operate more freely in both East and West. Detente has allowed environmental predators to make more money in more places without worrying about ideological adversarial voices in either of the IMF (International Monetary Fund) blocked in former blocs being able to mount an effective defensive campaign against them."

"Your saying, Yuri, that the basis of detente and glasnost and perestroika from the very beginning was for the interest of the powerful in getting both East and West to restructure and open themselves to their interests, while getting others to believe that it was in the interest of freedom and democracy for the powerless."

"Yes, that's correct. The idea was to allow a little freedom here and some democracy there as long as the powers to be in both East and West keep control of the profits to be in a new world order of greater freedom to economically control everyone."

"Yuri, your reason for being here is one for which I have the greatest respect; but others won't believe it and those in control won't want others to believe it."

"I'm aware of that, Vladimir, and that's why I've brought this document with me so that later, whether we live or die, they'll know why I was here. Just as you said, we're all unknown Vladimirs together, the righteous ones to save the world. And I want to show you these documents that I've arranged to be publicized in any future publicity about me. I want to remain unknown, like you do, so that my message will become widely known to the world. I'm laying my life on the line with you and with Yeltsin so that whether I live or die at these barricades, the world will know what I'll now let you know by reading this document to you. They'll listen, Vladimir, just like you want to listen, now, because everyone will listen to the words of a man who's willing to die for them.

"You're right Yuri, read it to me, please."

Lieutenant Yuri Mosyr reached under his shirt to remove a packet of papers from a pouch he carried strapped to his chest, unfolding the papers and turning on a battery powered light to read from them as follows:

"An International Ecological Forum of NGO (Non-Governmental Organizations) was held in Darlowo, Poland, from the 3rd to the 5th of May, 1991. A Professor Anatoli Jegorowicz Wolkow, a Member of the Parliament of Belorussia, Member of the Extraordinary Parliamentary Commission on Chernobyl and Head of the International Radiological Monitoring Laboratory was invited to address this forum. On the 4th of May after delivering his lecture, Professor Wolkow vanished."

"Dr. Jerry Jaskowski, a Polish medical doctor had invited Professor Wolkow to Poland in order to deliver a series of lectures entitled, Chernobyl Lessons, as a guest of the Second International Baltic Ecological Forum. The lectures were to be delivered first in Darlowo, and then in Gdansk, Poznan and finally Warsaw. These lectures were to be given in order to support the professor's activities in establishing an international laboratory in Belorussia to deal with the results of the nuclear disaster. Dr. Jaskowski had first met Professor Wolkow on the 28th of March, 1991, in Pinsk, Belorussia, which Dr. Jaskowski and two other scientists had visited at the invitation of the Belorussian Archbishop Kazimierz Swiatek in order to discuss future cooperation in studying the results of the Chernobyl nuclear accident. In reference to his lecture trip to Poland, Professor Wolkow had informed Dr. Jaskowski that he intended to spend all of his time in popularizing the problems of Chernobyl. Instead, he vanished."

"The document reports exactly how he vanished at the end, but first, let me give you the exact words and scientific data from his lecture," Yuri glanced up at him, as Vladimir nodded in encouragement for him to continue.

"I know the Chernobyl tragedy in detail. I have studied it from the very beginning and now I would like to present to all of you the material I have gathered as well as share my observations with you. It is for mankind never to forget what happened. The explosion in Chernobyl brought a lot of evil not only on our country but, I do not hesitate to say, on the whole world. What happened was the largest accident ever and what is more, this catastrophe has no end. Currently, 17 million people, 5 million children among them, are in danger. Our motherland is not able to cope with the problem by itself - it needs help from scientific circles all over the world."

"When on the 26th of April in the Center of the Polesie region, in the catchment area of the Prypec river this accident took place, I was present there in my capacity as a scientific ecological specialist. I know this region perfectly, it is very close to me because as a scientist I have been dealing with its ecology for 25 years. At the moment of the explosion and shortly after it, when the mass migration was in progress and everybody was trying to save his life, science was present there on the spot. One has to give answers to many questions immediately . . . and so it turned out that the reactor emitted not 50 min curie as was maintained, but about a milliard. A territory of 122,000 sq. km. is endangered, which is more or less a territory one and a half that of Austria. Neither today nor in the future will this area be able to serve man. Because of the contamination, clean production (healthy food) cannot be obtained there, nor should man live there."

"Survey monitoring of the endangered area is permanently carried out and it is already known today that we have to be prepared to remove people from where the contamination exceeds 5 to 10 curie. In Belorussia alone, 2 million people, among the a half million children are endangered. This land constitutes a living ecological training ground, and the question arises as to what to do with the people. After all, we cannot send them to the moon. This is an enormous problem that the world has never faced before."

"When it comes to the Chernobyl nuclear power plant, we scientists are of the opinion that it should not be working anymore. We have prepared a map of measurements in which the power plant contamination can be clearly seen: Caesium - 400 curie, Strontium - 100 curie, Plutonium - 10 curie per sq. km. I showed this map to the Director of the International Atomic Agency and his opinion was unequivocal - the nuclear power plant should be shut down at once."

"Table 1 presents the amount of Caesium in adult organisms. In 75% the amount of Caesium is from 1,000 to 8,000 pCi per gram potassium. In 6% to amount is from 20,000 to 70,000 pCi per gram potassium. None of the adults examined had the proper amount, and one should stress that radioactive Caesium does not exist in the natural state."

"The next two figures present data as to children. In Figure 1 one can see a report on the levels of contamination of school children in the village of Chojniki: - in the organisms of 52% of the children, a presence of 1,000 to 4,000 Bq. per gram potassium has been detected. In the organisms of 45% of those examined, there was respectively a presence of 500 to 1,000 Bq. per gram potassium; - contamination of the area with Strontium is 1.2 Ci per sq. km. All together, contamination of the area is 19.2 Ci per sq. km., which means that the whole population should most certainly be removed."

"There should be no radioactive Caesium in human organisms. Norms for people professionally exposed to radiation allow up to 40 Bq. per gram potassium."

"In Figure 2 the amount of Caesium in the organisms of school age children in the village of Tutgowice, Lomac and Lomysl is reported as follows:

- 1,000 to 4,000 Bq. per gram potassium in 43% of children;

- 4,000 to 8,000 Bq. per gram potassium in 42% of children;

- 8,000 to 70,000 Bq. per gram potassium in 12% of children."

"Contamination of the area with Strontium is 2.6 Ci per sq. km. while total contamination is 39.2 Ci per sq. km. The biological consequences are and continue to be tragic."

"Radioactive Caesium accumulated in human organisms and this fact has not been known to science until now. Our people had extinguished the fire of the 4th reactor, and one should realize that it is connected with the 3rd reactor - a common practice in Soviet nuclear power plants of sharing reactors for economic reasons."

"In the village of Omielkowszczina, 90% of the children were contaminated with Caesium 137 at over 1,200 pCi per gram potassium and 66% with over 2,000 pCi. In this village, there was not one child with the amount of Caesium lower than 800 pCi per gram potassium. The land contamination in the village was higher than 52 Ci per sq. km. and contamination of the surface with strontium itself was up to 1.0 Ci per sq. km."

Yuri stopped for a few moments to wipe the tears from his eyes, as he stated to Vladimir with his handkerchief to his eyes, "Omielkowszczina was my village, I was stationed here near Moscow with the Guards when the accident occurred, but my wife and son were there at home; my son will die soon and my wife a little later."

"I'm sorry, Yuri," was all he could say, at a loss for knowing what more he could say or do for such a loss as his.

"My family will die and maybe Ill die here, but this information will not die with me. By being here, and facing death with you, I'll be able to get others to face this kind of death, much worse than what we might face, and finally do something about it."

"Vladimir, let me continue and finish reading this to you."

"Certainly, Yuri."

"The nuclear power plant at Chernobyl is still working. Every day for the last five years about 4,000 people have been turning up to work there as if nothing has happened. The power plant is guarded by army forces of unknown numbers.'

"The Caesium contamination norm for the area is below O.1 curie per sq. km. The soil should not be contaminated either with strontium or plutonium. Radioactive plutonium is 10 million times more toxic than prussic acid used in gas chambers in concentration camps during the Second World War. Neither radioactive Caesium nor Strontium exists in nature in the natural state. Caesium, Strontium and Plutonium accumulate in living organisms; for example, in fish up to 50,000 times."

"Contamination of the coolant substance existing in the cooling installations of the Chernobyl power plant is up to 600 curie. It is three times more than in a similar faulty power plant in England. This means that the power plant is further contaminated while being cooled. The coolant will not only be contaminating the power plant but the Prypec river as well. Therefore, we've prepared maps of the Kiev water intake and all dams as far as the Black Sea. In Kiev, water intake there is 22,000 curie of radioisotopes. This means that the water intake has turned into a radioactive waste dump. Still it is used as a source of drinking water for Kiev."

"One can say that it was a miracle that the Black Sea has not been contaminated. It happened so because on the Prypec river there exists a complex system of water - power plant dams. If we do not immediately build sediment traps around Kiev, this complex dam system can get contaminated also. And this is the main southern complex supplying water to the Crimea. Its contamination is a threat to the existence of 40 million people living there. Please notice how big the range of the problem is."

"It turns out that contamination maps prepared by our scientific institutes do not show fully the whole extent of the problem. If we do not know the true estimation of the contamination territorial range, we make one mistake after another. For example, I will show you maps on which you can find the town of Sautycz. It's a new town established for the employees of the nuclear power plant. About 24,000 inhabitants, among them 6,000 children, live there. The cost of this town's construction was about 600 million rubles. According to our research, there is 10 to 20 curie Caesium contamination in this town. This means that we should remove all the inhabitants and simply build a new town on an uncontaminated area."

"Professor Wolkow was working on an extensive 10 part video tape series showing the effects of living in a contaminated area on children, on their state of health and psychological reactions as well. Consul Leonid Rodionow from the General Consulate of the Soviet Union in Gdansk attended the professor's first and last lecture. All the professor wanted to do was to scientifically report the facts and publicize the truth so that the world scientific community could work together on this problem. He concluded his lecture with the following recommendation:

'We should set up a center which would solve all problems in the contaminated zone, all the migration of radio uclices in this zone, then send this information via satellite into the universe and thus have a full control over the phenomena occurring there. We should also work out some technology which would allow us to use this vast land, with which nobody knows what to do today. Therefore, I am very anxious for this scientific knowledge and for all scientists to be engaged in working on this issue.

All people and especially children have to be examined systematically and currently.

Another important issue is in what way to get clean plant products. The whole world economics should consider this question. We have to use this lesson properly in case another disaster of this kind occurs. If not, we will bring the entire world to ruin.

In 1979 a similar core meltdown accident occurred in the nuclear power plant at Three Mile Island in Pennsylvania. At that time the nuclear industry spokesman announced that no contamination of the area took place. After 6 years the costs of eliminating the accident's consequences were 8 million in U.S. dollars which equals 160 million in rubles. In Belorussia, ladies and gentlemen, an area of 122,000 sq. km was contaminated.' "

Yuri looked up at Vladimir and continued to speak without reading, "This appeal of Professor Wolkow carried special weight in reference to his call for systematic monitoring of child victims, like my four year old son, because it had been discussed the year before in Gdansk."

"In November of 1990 at The First International Baltic Forum of NGOs[i], a motion was carried to organize medical teams to be sent to the area contaminated after the Chernobyl disaster. The basis for this motion was a report as to a 50% shortage of medical staff in the region. The result was an official invitation extended to Gdansk physicians by the Health Department in Pinsk through the mediation of Archbishop Kazimierz Swiatek. I know from the documents that at the meeting of the medical staff held at the Health Department in Pinsk on April 4th, all the technical details were agreed upon and the project was planned to start on the 24th of May. However, the medical team's visit was cancelled three days after Professor Wolkow was kidnapped."

"Kidnapped? How?"

"I'll go back to his arrival in Poland," Yuri replied, "and explain exactly how."

"Professor Wolkow was scheduled to meet with Dr. Jaskowski in Gdansk but arrived three days later than expected. When he did arrive he was met by the Russian Consul, Leonid Rodionow, who drove him to the symposium in Darlowo in his car. Rodionow informed Wolkow that General Dubinin urgently wanted to meet with him, as his colleague, at Legnica, to discuss some ecological problems that had occurred. Legnica is in an area occupied by the Soviet Army. After the professor delivered his lecture that I just read to you, he left with Rodionow in the Consul's car. They left, according to Dr. Jaskowski, for Legnica from whence the professor was to go to the Soviet Consulate in Gdansk at 7:00 p.m. the following day, May 5th. It was understood that Dr. Jaskowski was to meet Wolkow in Gdansk and accompany him to his home, where according to the original plans, he was to stay for his full time there."

"However, according to Consul Rodionow, they arrived in Gdansk at the Consulate where Professor Wolkow purportedly stayed overnight and from whence he departed for the Soviet Army stationing center in Borne-Sulimowo, the military airport, in the Koszalin District in a car sent by General Dubinin. Since then, the professor has not been seen, and he failed to appear at any of the planned lectures with an announcement being forwarded to the symposium organizers that Professor Wolkow had decided he'd fulfilled his duties and was now pursuing his private interests."

"It reminds one, doesn't it Vladimir, of Gorbachev's vacation rest in the Crimea."

"Yes, it certainly does."

"Three days after the Professor's disappearance, which was of course a kidnapping, Dr. Jaskowski, as coordinator of the symposium and head of the medical team that was to visit Belorussia, received a telegram from Archbishop Swiatek which I'll read to you:

'Health Department in Pinsk informed me that it cancelled the trip of Polish physicians from Gdansk. No comment!"

"Whether Professor Wolkow is ever heard from again, I'm here for my son and millions of other children to make sure that our struggle for environmental survived is heard around the world."

"Nobody, Vladimir, wanted to go near this case. Neither the Americans nor the Swedes, both of whom were contacted, would touch it. The Americans were reluctant to embarrass Gorbachev, and the Swedes were fearful of the KGB in their backyard."

"Wasn't it an American President who said the only thing we have to fear is fear itself?"

"I think it was Roosevelt, Yuri."

"Well, I'm not afraid of them, even if the Americans, the Swedes and the Germans and the rest of Europe are. An American may have phrased it right, but I'll show them how it's done right."

"That's why I'm here, with you as Vladimir, for my fight for my son and for all children."

"Yuri, you're right, and it is your fight, and you're right in another way also."

"How's that?"

"It's our fight today and it will be the world's fight tomorrow," Vladimir replied, as he climbed out of the tank to go to the next tank.

He spent the entire might talking with each of the First Lieutenants who'd come with their tank crews to choose to stand with him in defense of the Russian White House. Every one of them, like Lieutenant Mosyr from Belorussia had a personal reason for being there that went far beyond the call for democracy. The barricades for political democracy were seen by each of these tank commanders as the beginning of an irreversible momentum upwards for their own personal and higher causes.

First Lieutenant Peter Budris from Lithuania was the next man he spoke with. His explanation was the most obvious and the easiest to understand. Very simply, his country was stolen in a Hitler - Stalin pact maintained by a Gorbachev - Bush pact.

When the Stalinists ruled, it was the order of the day for those in the West to rest while speaking about Baltic freedom, in knowing that nothing would happen. Ironically, when Gorbachev first announced a new day of freedom and self-determination in a new world order, it became the new order of the day to put Baltic freedom last just when the first possibility for it to happen saw the light of day.

Gorbachev sullied his noble peace with his ignoble surprise omen for freedom, of an Omon of Black Berets against freedom, an omen to every democratic demonstrator in every republic in the Soviet Union. This ignoble black beret death in the slaughter of democratic demonstrators in Vilnius during January of 1991 remained a "Vilenius Vile" legacy and threat to those on the barricades of freedom, now, just seven months later.

Unfortunately, not only did Gorbachev sell out and fail to meet his mortgage on his common European House, but the Bush league, as well, sold out on foreclosing upon uncommon national freedom in selling out to common Soviet business. Just as Kissinkick's "Ass" Associates dropkicked freedom to Chinese fat ass, American ideals of freedom lost to deals such as the Soviet-American pact of a pat business deal tailor made for fat cat Soviet and American fat asses.

Yet, while all of this was quite obvious, there remained one strange anomaly concerning the intrigues of the leading asses of Kissinkicks Associates, Brent Socrafty and Lawrence Eataburger the 3rd helping. Namely, why did Socrafty earn only $500,000 per year compared to Eataburger's one million dollars. This mystery stumped both the CIA and the KGB and remained a source of consternation worldwide, leaving many a sleepless night in Bonn, Paris and London, until it was solved one day by a fast food worker at Burger King. It was discovered that so skinny Socrafty never eats burgers while Eataburger eats so many third helpings that an extra $500,000. was allocated to Eataburger's supplemental cost of living by burgers account. Burger King quickly leaked their analysis to the oxymoron intelligence community that they needed to pay much more attention to Eataburger. The CIA subsequently made Eataburger their primary Central Intelligence Ass; and since Eataburger was a smart ass, they ordered extra burgers from Burger King to be distributed to all of their CIA special Ass assets in creating more smart asses.

"Vladimir," Lieutenant Budris stated, "I'm here to fight in order to prevent what happened to my people."

"In some way your fight has already begun," he replied.

"In what way?"

"In the way that so many Russians might not have had the courage to stand on barricades and defend a democratic chance for the future, if your people hadn't shown the way first."

"In that sense you're right, but the price of freedom is never free and a number of Lithuanians paid with their lives. I'm here with you to make sure that if these people on the barricades have to pay with their lives, Omon will pay as well."

"I don't think they'll deploy Omon against them," he responded, "at least not as long as we're here; but they're more likely to use the Alpha Group."

Vladimir went on to explain the new threat facing them in response to which Lieutenant Peter Budris replied, "If that's it, I prefer to go out with a bang, but I can assure you I'll blast some of them back to every oblast (county) in their hell of a Soviet Union."

"I'm sure you will. You're one of the best marksmen in the Guards, and I'm also sure you won't be seeing them in hell."

"That's right, Vladimir, I intend as a good Catholic boy to go directly upstairs to my namesake's entrance, St. Peter's heavenly gate."

"When we get inside the gate, we'll drink some vodka up there and celebrate with the first round on you," Vladimir stated, with mock seriousness.

"The first round is on me, but all the rest are on you and they'll be a lot of them," Peter responded, as if they both assumed that an omniscient God would certainly know enough to stock heaven with plenty of Russian vodka if nothing else.

The next First Lieutenant, Islam Ayat from Kazakhstan, while also a candidate for admission to an ecumenical heaven was less likely as a Muslim to join in with a Nazdrovia to vodka - no matter how heavenly. His province had declared sovereignty in October of 1990 only after 13 other republics had done so. It's President, Nursultan Nazarbayev, who'd resigned from the Politburo and Central Committee to protest the coup, still hoped for a new union treaty to create a commonwealth of republics. Of the approximately 17 million people in Kazakhstan, almost 7 million of whom were Russians along with slightly more than one million ethnic Germans and slightly less than one million Ukrainians, the Muslim Kazaks found themselves outnumbered in their own republic.

"I'm here," Islam explained to Vladimir, "because I want to protect my freedom for my religion away from the atheism of the Soviet north and away from the Islamic fundamentalism of the south."

"If we can stay together in some kind of cooperative economic union, we can transport what we produce to Russia and receive what we need in return. If not, we'll fall further behind and become more ingrown, praying to Allah as we fall prey to conflict among ourselves. The first popular upheaval in the Soviet Union under Gorbachev's government occurred in our capital, Alma Ata, in 1986, when the Party appointment of an ethnic Russian to replace Dinmukhamed Kunaev sparked three days of rioting."

"With an underdeveloped economy and economic dependence on subsidies, our chances for real independence are not very good. In addition to the prospects of growing unemployment for our unskilled labor force, ethnic tensions in our mixed population are being aggravated by scarce water and grazing lands. Along with the other Central Asian Republics, we have the highest rates of population growth in the Soviet Union. In effect, we're a Muslim tinderbox ripe for an Islamic explosion. With the memory of Afghanistan still making many Russians nights a nightmare, it's a certainly that should the explosion come, no one from outside or inside will be able to put out the fire."

"Then, Islam, you're here to fight for a nation with Muslims against the alternatives of a Muslim nation for Muslims or a Communist nation for Communists."

"That's absolutely correct, for fundamentalism in any religion - Marxist, Muslim, Christian or Jewish - is fundamental in the respect that it destroys the fundamentals of human decency for others. We had and still have our Jihad Soldiers of God who love death. Latin Christians murdered Muslims, Jews and Byzantine Christians in the name of a loving Savior. Jews have their West Bank settlers, who settle God's promises to themselves as victims in denying the promise of God to all men, in victimizing Palestinians as a people who don't even exist."

"Your right, Islam, but I'm afraid our Christian fundamentalism didn't die in the cruel Crusades as it should have. We observed a tragic illustration of it in Northern Ireland where Protestant fundamentalists, who believe in an infallible Bible, attacked Catholics, some of whom are fundamentalist in believing in an infallible Church. In what used to be called Yugoslavia, Orthodox Christian Serbs attacked Catholic Croats and Bosnian Muslims, with all sides justifying hatred for the other based on their mutual fundamentalist sins of the past."

"Vladimir, you can see very well what I'm fighting for and against. It just occurred to me from what you were saying that the Serbs could better serve themselves in seeing how they can serve peace instead of a Greater Serbia - which means lesser for others."

"I totally agree with you, Islam, and if they don't, I'm afraid that many of the Slavic peoples in Yugoslavia and the rest of Eastern Europe will make their Slavic lands into a future pan - Slavic 'slave' area for themselves. In so doing, it will be their own undoing, in their own making of their early Roman slave designation of themselves as Slavs!"

"Did you know, Vladimir, that our republic's development advisor is a Korean."

"No, I didn't".

"I wondered about that myself and hoped that maybe a Korean Buddhist could help us become Buddies - Muslims, Christian, and Jews - to be Seoul brothers together. I would have included Marxists, but, unlike the Marx Brothers, they're not very funny and no one wants them as friends anymore."

"Islam, no matter where Seoul might be politically, or where our souls might be religiously, I'd be proud for you to consider me your Soul brother."

"Soul brother it is!"

He left Islam feeling more and more like a real soul man, a man who was finding his real soul in finding the soul of others.

The next tank he went to was commanded by First Lieutenant Valery Mosiyak of the Ukraine. With a population of approximately fifty two million people, substantial industry and abundant agriculture, the Ukraine had a real chance of not only going it alone, but making it alone. Having lost seven million of its people to a Stalinist forced famine and many others since who'd dared to speak out against Moscow, the prevailing policy could best be characterized as that of a permanent disunion of the Ukraine from the Soviet Union.

"Lieutenant Mosiyak, I'm grateful you're with us. For a while I was worried that a Ukrainian would consider a Russian as the first person to fight against and the last to fight with."

"Vladimir, I pray that Russians and Ukrainians will never fight each other again."

"I'll pray to that as well. With four and a half million Ukrainians living in Russia and eleven million Russians living in the Ukraine, such a fight would destroy both of our peoples."

"I'm here to fight for something else, Vladimir, something that involves both Russia and the Ukraine and others."

"I'm with you, Valery, as long as we can continue to fight together."

"Yes, we can. I'm here to put an end to nuclear politics before it puts an end to us."

"I don't like nuclear weapons anymore than you do, but how can we put an end to nuclear politics?"

"We can stop it by using this opportunity for freedom from central control to freedom from all nuclear weapons."

"I like your idea, but I don't see how it can be done."

"I'll explain how by explaining what's happening in the Ukraine, what's likely to happen and what can happen if we make it happen."

"Please do."

"Because of our stand here together, the Union structure, the Soviet center, is doomed. In a short time you'll hear politicians like

Vladimir Grinev, Deputy Speaker of the Ukrainian legislature and a Russian, himself, speak out categorically and definitively against any union structure and presidency as well as any other remnant of the center to specifically include the Supreme Soviet."

"But Grinev has gone on record as being in favor of keeping a stable ruble for the Ukraine."

"Yes, that's correct in that he wants to keep the ruble from going to rubble. That economic arrangement, however, is only for the purpose of maintaining an economic agreement with other republics, not an economic association."

"Further, I predict that we'll soon see old communist party deck hands quickly changing their colors and jumping on the deck of the new good ship Ukrainian nationalism. Someone like Leonid Kravchuk, a communist party official in charge of ideology will be among the first. In fact, I predict that Kravchuk will literally chuk his Marxism for Nationalism rather than deal with democratic reformers in Moscow.

"You certainly know the Ukraine better than I do, but still, I don't see the nuclear factors."

"It's coming, Vladimir, as the next step from what I'll describe. George H. Bush visited the Ukraine just a few months ago, and instead of encouraging national freedom, as not only the Rukh nationalists hoped for but as most Ukrainians assumed, he delivered his Chicken Kiev speech warning us Ukes, in Bush league fashion, about the dangers of our own need for national freedom. Feeling powerless and likely to be abandoned to the Soviet - American center, Ukraine decided to use its one trump card that not even a Donald Trump would dare or be foolish enough to gamble with - its nuclear arsenal.

"Valery, it seems as if the Bush league you've described speaks loudly about the freedom of nations in its call for a new world order, but keeps numb wherever there's a real issue of freedom in nations."

"That's exactly what I'm saying, but the rules of the game have now changed in the Ukraine. Unlike the Balts, who were relegated to obscurity by the Soviet - American center, there are a large number of nuclear weapons in the possession of the Ukraine; and everyone in the world is nervous about that fact, as they should be. However, the nuclear politics comes in when a republic such as the Ukraine - and there are others with nuclear weapons - decides to put its political agenda on the table with its nuclear weapons."

"Here is the nuclear political development I see as possible, even probable, unless the whole world becomes a nuclear free zone. The Ukraine authorizes an independent army, numbering about 400,000 men. The declare their republic to be a nuclear state in order to gain nuclear political parity with the Soviet Union as the center that they want to negotiate themselves away from. Further, they use this nuclear political strategy as the impetus for obtaining international recognition along with full military autonomy and mobilization."

"Very simply, Valery, you envision nuclear politics as the utilization of the issue of nuclear weapons for political ends."

"Yes, and if nuclear politics succeeds once, which it may do in the Ukraine, it can easily spread not only to other former Soviet republics but to every big and little Sad damn dictator. For every extremist group in the world with a political agenda, the more attractive, strategic, and even necessary, nuclear politics becomes."

"Just imagine Vladimir, if Azerbaijan and Armenia had what the Ukraine could have, with their own armies and nuclear arsenals, in their conflict over the Nagorny - Karabakh area."

"I see your point, Valery."

"And just imagine, if you will, a world with dozens or very possibly hundreds and eventually, even thousands of similar situations."

"I can imagine it, but I don't want to."

"I don't want to either, that's why I'm with you to fight for legitimate autonomy, self-determination, free electrons and full democracy. I want to show the world that a few men called Vladimir, a few righteous unknown men as you described us, can make a difference that the whole world will know. I'll fight where necessary and whether I win now or win later, I'm doing it for a world where the possession of any nuclear weapon held by the largest center to the smallest group becomes internationally illegal as a crime against humanity."

"Vladimir, you described this new neutron weapon in letting me choose to stay or leave. I have one clear choice and that is to stay. If they kill me with their new weapon, maybe, by God, they'll finally have to face themselves and decide to end this proliferating nuclear obscenity, which with all our scientific ingenuity we've now made available to individuals at the squad level."

"I don't want to die, Vladimir, but if I must, there's no better cause to die for."

"I hope we don't die, Valery, but as long as we're alive, you've shown me a cause there's nothing better to live for."

He left Lieutenant Valery Mosiyak for the next tank, realizing that each of these men were showing him more about how to choose to live than to die.

First Lieutenant Andrei Adrinian from Armenia was the leader of the next tank he visited. As an Armenian, he knew well the tragic legacy in man's history of the blood feuds of one's religion and nation. The Christian Armenians had most recently been fighting their Muslim neighbor Azerbaijan since 1988, when in that year the Armenian enclave of Nagorno-Karabakh voted to secede from Azerbaijan. The silent world reaction to the Armenian holocaust at the hands of the Turks has been credited with providing Adolph Hitler with the historical precedent to assume he could succeed with a Jewish holocaust without any serious world opposition - an assumption that proved to be as accurate as it was perfidious.

Once again the world stood back as the crumbling walls of communism revealed the old walls of ethnic and religious hate - no where more intransigent than here. Instead of growing together as individuals in freedom, the proclivity to grow apart in hatred and group tension was a past, present and future tense problem. Conflict between Armenians and their Moslem neighbors was a past tense reality with Turks, a present tense problem with Azeris, and a future tense tension with Iranians.

Vladimir explained the situation to Adrinian and the threat they faced from the new weaponry with a certain matter of factness that surprised even himself. Most civilians are initially awed or horrified by the emotionless aplomb with which professional soldiers and the police (in American cities they're synonymous) recount mayhem and death. Rather than concluding that these apparently calloused professionals have become dehumanized by their profession, the better explanation is that an outward desensitization is developed in order to protect and nurture any remnant of emotional vulnerability remaining deep inside them. Lieutenant Andrei Adrinian knew enough of war, group conflict and hate to see beyond what Vladimir was saying to what he was feeling.

"Vladimir, you and I have something in common in that there are 425,000 Russians living in Azerbaijan, almost exactly the same number as Armenians living there. Many of my people have already fled in the wake of pogroms and, very possibly, the same could happen to Russians in the future. Unlike some other republics, historically we've looked to Russia as a protector from our neighboring but not very neighborly Islamic world. The Azeri nationalists would like to unite with their kin in Iran, and Armenians have as much trust of Turks that Jews have of Germans, with much more reason for skepticism.

"I know Adrinian that the situation has deteriorated with Armenians fleeing Azerbaijan and Azeris fleeing Armenia."

"I chose to come and defend this Russian White House with you because I believe that individual freedom and political democratic compromise can overcome groupism: which I describe as a process of identifying one's self and one's goals through one's group."

"But Andrei, ethnic and group identity will never disappear. Just look at that over two hundred year old ethnic melting pot experiment known as America and you can see two historically victimized groups, Jews and Blacks, victimizing one another today by fighting each other in the streets of New York City.

"Vladimir, I don't pretend that ethnic and national and religious identities can or even should disappear; but what I am saying is that without new ways of bringing different peoples together, our national melting pots will turn into national core meltdowns.

"I agree with you."

"The new coup," Andrei continued to speak, "made the old mistake of trying to solve a problem by thinking that through central power and dictates they could control it. While it's possible to keep the lid on for a while, eventually the problem just simmers and boils over sooner or later at a scorching temperature. Gorbachev, although pointed in the right direction with his reforms, never really stepped out and did anything. He basically ignored group conflicts until the riot troops had to be called out to stem the bloodshed."

"I'd agree with you on that as well."

"The answer for us Armenians, Azeris, Russians, and everyone else is to develop democratic mechanisms that allow us the freedom to grow apart and to grow together as both individuals and as members of different groups without groupism. The answer, simply, is political democratic compromise: and that's what you and me and all of us here, we Vladimirs, together represent. If we survive, I intend to take our stand here at these barricades as a stand for dismantling barricades between people."

"I'll say Amen, Be It So to that!"

"My first proposal is going to be to Boris Yeltsin that he personally go to Nagorno-Karabakh and work out a democratic political compromise."

"I think he'll go, Andrei."

"Yes, I think he will also."

"Maybe," Vladimir suggested, "he can get Azerbaijan to agree to full autonomy for the Armenians in the Nagorny- Karabakh region if they accept for the time being the political status quo of their region remaining within Azerbaijan."

"You see," Andrei replied smiling, "the solutions aren't complex; the next fight to win is a comparatively simple one - simply the will to stop fighting."

"Andrei," Vladimir spoke, as he turned to climb out of the tank, "after listening to your reason for being here, I have a new reason for fighting the coup - to fight them for a way to stop us from fighting."

With more certitude about his own reason in listening to the reasons of these men, he approached the next tank commanded by First Lieutenant Janis Kaza of Latvia.

The Baltic republic of Latvia with a population slightly under 3 million, of whom only 52% were Latvians, faced many daunting problems. With few natural resources and few products good enough for export to the West, and with a lack of hard currency to pay for necessary imports on the world market, little Latvia had some very big problems. Further, while Lithuania could barter food for increasingly expensive Russian oil, Latvia was not able to do so since it didn't produce even enough grain to feed itself.

Knowing these overwhelming problems, Vladimir was stunned to encounter a smiling and cheerful Lieutenant Janis Kaza, appearing to be more confident then anyone he'd encountered today, including himself. When he explained their predicament and related the weapons threat they were facing, Lieutenant Kaza shrugged it off as if he were shooing away an annoying wasp.

"Vladimir, ever since the Second World War, we Latvians have lived with its consequences. Our capital Riga was an example to the world as to how Soviet Rigamortis kills individual initiative and denies the chance at human living that goes with one's freedom. Finally, today, what has been done to us is being undone by us with the vision of freedom giving new life to our nation's freedom. I know that, economically, we should be running to Moscow on our hands and knees for the old oil way of getting by; and I know that with our freedom, it'll be very tough to get by. I know our economic facts of life, but I'm here to fight the coup because I prefer living with the fact of our freedom."

"Janis, I must say that I admire you in that in knowing the predicament of your nation's situation, you still prefer the unknowing predicament of your nation's freedom."

"Yes I do, for I'd rather live in a small nation in a big world of freedom than live in a small world of big nations with little freedom."

He left Janis Kaza of Latvia realizing that he had little to say to him and much to learn from him about freedom.

"The next tank was commanded by First Lieutenant Viktor Kuznetsov from Leningrad, soon to be the new old St. Petersburg. Lieutenant Kuznetsov had been converted back to the orthodox religion of his forbearers by a Muscovite Russian Orthodox priest of Jewish descent. That priest, Father Alexander Men, was murdered with an axe in the autumn of 1990, just days before he was to become the first Theological lecturer since the revolution at a state pedagogical center in Moscow. Father Men, a true Judeo-Christian, even in the ethnic sense, was axed for the socialist crime of preaching a social justice that found international socialism to be less than just. Vladimir explained their situation and the threat facing them to which Viktor responded:

"As a believer, I believe that all things happen for the good for those that love the Lord. I was a member of Father Men's congregation until he was murdered for his message of grace in a coup de grace by the very same people who are now trying to murder Russia with their coup d'etat. Father Men died for us and if it is my fate to die for Russia, then my faith will give me the courage to accept my fate."

Viktor Kuznetsov represented a new trend in Russia, that of Russian Orthodox believers who believed in the future even more than the past. He'd come to this belief in combining the traditions of Russia's religious past with the visions of its new religious visionaries like Father Men. He fused religious tradition and vision with charismatic Christians, who were infusing a new Pentecostal charisma into the old icons of the Russian Orthodox Church.

Like any true believer who believes in truth, one who combines the best of the old in adjusting to the new, he looked back to face what's within in order to go forward in facing up to the future. The distinction between an old time religion and an all time religion is that the former reacts with an old faith in a worse future, while the latter climbs up to the best of the present with a new faith in unlimited possibility for the future limited only by the wisdom of its past.

"Vladimir, did you see the film Repentance by Tengiz Abuladze?"

"No, not yet."

"Well, after we've given our own coup de grace to this coup d'etat, would you promise me to see it in return for my accompanying you as one of your unknown Vladimirs to save what we know of this world."

"That's the very least I can and will do."

"In 1988 I attended the millennial celebration of Russian Christianity and discovered that Mikhail Gorbachev, whose mother is an Orthodox believer, and Raisa Gorbachev have been in close contact with Dmitry Likbachev, the major Christian scholar on the culture of Old Russia. Also, I've learned that Boris Yeltsin had his grandchildren baptized and chose a confessing Christian general as his running mate in the presidential campaign in the Russian republic. Everywhere you turn you can see new movements such as the Society for Open Christianity, founded by Mikhail Kazachkov, who's well know for his long-time independent stand as a political prisoner. Inside Russia we're seeing the growth in just a few years of the urban diocese of Nizhni-Novgorod from two to ten churches along with a mosque and a synagogue. In Sverdlovsk, there are now five churches where just a short time ago there was only one. I'm here to fight to defend this new freedom of religion, and when I fight because of my religious faith, I'll fight with a spiritual attitude."

"And what, pray tell, is a spiritual attitude?"

"I'll fight with an attitude of love, strange as it may sound."

"You sound a lot like Jesus who taught his followers to love thine enemy, didn't he?"

"Yes he did, Vladimir, and I feel blessed to be on the barricades between light and darkness with a Russian who knows something about Jesus!"

"Praise the Lord," Vladimir responded, in a proclamation of belief in an attempt to try to make it easier for Viktor, but also, in an attempt to make it easier for himself, in trying to believe for himself, as well as in himself.

"Vladimir, I know from what I believe that Jesus was right about the power of fear being overcome by the power of love. Eventually something new will happen to the world and that's real Christianity; but before that can happen to others, Christianity first has to become real to Christians.

"Viktor, from what you've said, it occurred to me that non-Christians are offended not by Jesus Christ but by Me First Christians, who in preaching Jesus as first in God's sight, never cease to get out of sight in putting themselves first."

"You're right, perhaps we should consider using a different name since official Christianity has failed real Christianity so often that people assume Jesus Christ failed."

"I have a new word for you, instead of Christianity, I propose Jesusanity - meaning Jesus as the way to sanity."

"Father Men would be proud of you, Vladimir. It's true that Christianity is false on the outside if Jesus isn't truly inside, and that without Jesus life is spiritually insane. I asked you if you'd seen Repentance, which is the best artistic work of the Gorbachev period. The same word, repentance, appears in the titles of new independent journals and in the theme of the new museum of Soviet history, the Museum of the Young Communist League in Sverdlovsk."

"Repent and sin no more is certainly a sermon the coup should have listened to," Vladimir replied.

"They and hopefully others will be converted because of what we're doing as our penance for democracy, in making a public contrition with our tanks for their sins against freedom. We may be militarily crucified, you and me and all of us, but what we're doing will redeem others in giving them an example of how to heal themselves by repenting of communism in turning away from the sins of the coup."

"Even though you walk through the valley of death," Viktor continued to speak, "go in peace and fear not."

He left Viktor's tank reconverted by Viktor's faith.

It occurred to him as he climbed down from the tank that Viktor had the spiritual insight to determine the nature of the thirty sixth unknown righteous man, who was still unknown not only to the world but to himself. This last righteous man could be righteous to the degree that he would overcome fear of others and, most importantly, fear of himself in finding the right strength in fighting the wrong power.

The next tank he approached was commanded by First Lieutenant Igor Aksyonov, like Viktor a Russian in every respect but unlike him in every other respect. Lieutenant Aksyonov came to fight for a Russian nation free for Russians alone, whereas Viktor was there to fight for the nation of Russia as a free nation for all. The difference between them being most significant in their different attitude toward non-Russians and most particularly the Jew. Viktor was happy to see the Jews along with Muslims and Christians free to be themselves, whereas Igor was happiest in seeing Jews leave Russia with one way tickets to anywhere else.

Vladimir explained their situation and threat to Igor who, surprisingly, responded by blaming the Jews.

"I'm here to make sure that the Jews who started Bolshevism in Russia don't get away with the pretense that they're now so-called democrats and reformers with something to say about Russia's future. This fight is the first fight against the coup, but the second fight against the Jew will be the real fight for Russian freedom."

It was quite evident that Igor was a member of Pamyat, meaning memory, a Russian organization that championed pure, old, agrarian Russian virtues against the corrupt values of the West and the corruption of minorities - most of all the Jew.

"Send the Yids home to their leader, Shitsack Shamir and let them stay in their foreign *Sinagogues* instead of staying here and polluting Russia. Everyone in the world knows that real Russians, like your father and mine, were the heroes who fought and died in World War II. Yet, all one hears in the media is the Hollywood *Holohoax* of six million Jews. Lenin might have been the leader of the Bolsheviks, but the Jews were his officers. Of the leading Commissars, Trotsky, Zinovieff, Kameneff, Stekloff, Sverdloff, Uritsky, Joffe, Rekovsky, Radek, Menjinsky, Larin, Bronski, Zaalkind, Volodarsky, Petroff, Litvinoff, Smidovitch and Vororsky were each and every one Jews."

"Igor, like yourself, I consider myself a real Russian and I'd like to be a Russian patriot, but I don't think blaming Jews for the past or present is going to help us build our future."

"Vladimir, while you're a man of good intentions, unfortunately you're very naive. Just look at the facts. Marx himself, born Mordechai Levy, was a Jew and his teacher, Moyshe Gess, was a Jew who infected his mind with communist ideas. Lenin was partly Jewish from his mother's side and Trotsky was a Jew. Brezhnev's real name was Garbinski and his wife's maiden name was Goldbery; Jews not only killed our Tsar but, likewise, murdered the Russian people by means of a Jew administered system of collectivization, executions and gulags. The world renowned mathematician, Igor Shafarevich, has attributed this scourge to the vengeful sentiments taught to Jews by their Talmud, what I call a Tallmud of tall tales and mud. Anatolyi Smirnov, as a spokesman for Pamyat, has documented that of 540 officials in leading positions after the October Revolution, 490 were Jews."

"Igor, undoubtedly some Jews, even many Jews supported Communism in a mistakes belief that it might remedy some social injustices. It's true we've been persecuted by Stalinism, but Stalin was a Georgian, not a Jew, and we have to face the fact that we brought Communism on ourselves. As Russians we have a double-indemnity persecution complex in that while we've been persecuted by this system, we also created our own Russo-centric persecution of ourselves. Blaming everything on the Jews is a way to escape accepting any blame for ourselves."

"Do you love your country?" Igor asked.

"Yes I do."

"Then, you're a potential member of Pamyat," he almost shouted out.

"No, I'm not," Vladimir quietly, but definitively, responded.

Igor's question reminded him of an encounter he'd experienced in accepting an invitation from a fellow officer last year to visit the headquarters of Pamyat, the National Patriotic Front, located in an old house on Volova Street in Moscow. As he entered the building he recalled being confronted by a cloth banner proclaiming, "Christ is Resurrected," in old Russian Cyrillic lettering. A picture of St. Gregory, Father of the Church, hung next to a Star of David with a skull and cross-bones affixed inside it. He was greeted by a young man in a commando uniform who read out a slogan that had been nailed onto the wall over his head to read: "They Need a Major Shake-up. We Need a Great Russia." This statement originally came from Tsar Nicolas II's minister of internal affairs, Stolypin, who later became prime minister. "Stolypin was Russia's savior," the young commando announced, "who was assassinated in 1920 by a Jew, Mortka Bogorov. We know who's been scheming against Russia and we know who needs the shake-up."

Founded by Dmitri Dmiryevich Vasilyev, Pamyat, with branches in 40 cities and rapidly expanding contacts in Germany and the United States, publishes a monthly magazine whose masthead reads, "Patriots of the World Unite! In the name of the Tsar and Mother Russia."

A Pamyat activist was tried and sentenced to two years imprisonment for shouting racist slogans at a meeting of the Union of Soviet Writers, and a leader of Pamyat was recently assassinated. Both of these attempts to fight it have, in creating martyrs, had the complete opposite effect in bringing hundreds of thousands of new members into its fold. A candidate for Pamyat membership is required to supply three addresses of Jews to complete his application. This organization has extensive files of all members of the Soviet establishment, with lists of their true Jewish names replete with their family genealogy three to four generations back. They have a Who's Who of Hidden Jews that would astound any genealogical archivist.

In their magazine, deformed hooked-nosed Semites are trampled upon by strong Russian Knights displaying attractive Slavic features, and Jewish dwarfs are depicted as destroying mosques with dynamite. In one of their poems entitled, "Infidels," a picture of a Zionist Soviet press run by men with crooked fingers displaying Star of David tattoos is captioned with the statement, "We'll trample you as we would trample dirt. We are no longer afraid of death."

"It's not we the Slavs, Sergei Vasilyev, the 33 year old son of Pamyat's founder stated, who have brought Communism to the world."

"My long and painstaking analysis of Russian history has revealed to me the truth about the Jewish plot. Soviet means Freemason. Communism is the work of a sect; no major difference exists between Communism and the Jewish religion. We want to make nations aware of their patriotic duties. We want a monarchy for Russia, which is the single form of government that has not been destroyed by the Zionist - Freemason sect. Pamyat is the heir of all those who fought against these sects."

Ironically or perhaps not, Pamyat surfaced on October 4, 1985, the same year that Gorbachev introduced glasnost and perestroika. While apparently an irony in that one postures an open brave new world for the future and the other proffers a closed grave new world of the past, perhaps it is less ironic and most predictable that freedom can be a two edged dangerous sword.

Together, Igor and Vladimir were fighting against both lousey - failed communism and lousey - faire capitalism in fighting against the coup. However, they would never be together in what they were fighting for. As he left Igor, he realized that there is only one personal mistake and political error more damning that that of doing the wrong thing for the right reason; and that is the damnable and unmistakable error of doing what Igor had done in doing the right thing in fighting the coup for the wrong reason.

The next tank he approached was commanded by the first officer to volunteer, Lieutenant Israel Horowitz. As he went over to talk with him he could not but shutter at the distance of the gulf separating Igor and Israel, which gulf constituted a greater future Gulf War between the two of them who were greater enemies to each other than they were to the coup. Israel Horowitz, he knew, had his own special reasons for being here and no one, not even Igor, could ever accuse him of being naive.

"Welcome back, Vladimir, Lieutenant Budris has already spoken to me about the threat we face, and I must tell you that I'd think less of you if you harbored any suspicious that I might leave."

"Israel, you're spared me having to explain our situation yet again; and in reference to any suspicion of your leaving, I know from the beginning that you'd be the last to leave."

"How did you know that?"

"That's a good question, I don't know how I knew it, but I know it."

"Well my good friend, from one Vladimir to another, you know right!"

"Then, Israel, would you mind telling me why I was right."

"Certainly I'll tell you. First, I'm a Jew in case you couldn't guess from my name, and I know too well what some Russians think about us Jews."

"I also know, Israel, and I'm afraid some of those Russians are not only out there against us, but here with us."

"I'm not surprised for I expected it, and that's why I made damn sure that I was here too."

"Well, I'm damn glad that you're here, whatever your reason."

"Vladimir, I'd like you to be glad for the reasons I came as well as for the fact that I'm here."

"Tell me, Israel, and I'll tell you."

"I know some Jews did Stalin's dirty work, but people forget about how the Jews suffered under Communism with everyone else. In some ways we experienced less of a holocaust, but more of a double whammy persecution from Communism than Nazism, in that we not only had our religion destroyed by the Communists but, in addition, we were blamed by the Russian Christians for the fact that Communists persecuted them."

"You're saying that, on one hand, Jews suffered for being believing Jews and, on the other hand, they suffered because some Jews weren't believing Jews but believing Communists."

"Yes, we got it from the religious and the atheists alike. It seems as if no matter what some of us do or don't do, some group is out to blame us for anything they see as wrong. Jesus was a Jew who started a Judeo-Christian sect leading to Christianity, in response to which early Jews who liked Jesus were persecuted by Jews and Gentiles alike. Later, Gentile Christianity brought pogroms to Jews in the name of their anti-Jew, Jewish Messiah. In the Final Solution of the Holocaust, Jews were held guilty not only for Judaism and Communism, but for Jewish originated Christianity as well.

"If there's one aspect of human nature that we've experienced in our history more than any other people, it's man's tendency to debase himself by victimizing others in the name of a superior definition of one's own group in reference to another. Some of our own people, most tragically, have shown that Jews are no different from other people in victimizing Palestinians in their own Nazi Flashback to having been victimized themselves. In reference to our own ethno-centric Judeo-Nazis, for the first time in my life, I prayed that a group of minority Jews remain in a minority position."

"I suppose," Vladimir replied, "their activities shouldn't surprise anyone who doesn't think Jews are any better or worse than anyone else."

"It shouldn't surprise anyone unless one thinks that one group is superior, and another inferior, which automatically qualifies one as a victimizer. The main cause of the classic victimization of Jews has been group stereotyping, where because of the misdeeds of one Jew, the rest of us suffer. Imagine if one Russian steals something and, from thenceforward, all Russians are characterized as thieves."

"That reminds me, Israel, of an American comedian I once heard when I was in the States, by the name of Jackie Mason, who complained about anti-Semitism as being unfair in that it deprived Jews of the right to be judged by their individual demerits."

"Yes, that's a funny form of comic relief, but what we need immediate relief from is, I'm afraid, no where near as funny as Jackie Mason's comedy. So many Jews not only in the Soviet Union but in the United States, as well, have changed their names in the hope of appearing not to be Jewish. At times, that's been necessary in order to escape persecution, but notice that my name is clearly a Jewish one."

"That's for sure, Israel."

"And I'm here to fight for my meaning of freedom and democracy to mean that every person, Jew and non-Jew alike, should present himself for what he is, to be accepted for the person he is, and to be proud of who he is."

"For all it may mean to you, Israel, I'm very proud to be here with you not as a Russian Jew but as a Russian and a Jew."

"It means everything to me, and it would mean everything to whatever new freedom we're fighting for, if everyone were like you and me in reference to each other."

"Israel, all of us have to protect our identity, now, by being unknown Vladimirs. But when we beat this coup, I want to make sure that no individual ever again - Jew or Gentile - has to be known as Vladimir in order to protect himself."

It was now over and not yet begun. The moment had passed for the truth to begin in facing life and death in the name of what was right in what they were doing. There was no guarantee with freedom that a free choice would guarantee that it would be the right choice, only that the right way to freedom begins with the right choice.

CHAPTER EIGHTEEN

Groupism and the Perfection of Evil

Vladimir reflected on the reasons for these men doing the righteous thing in the name of their respective causes. He felt that Igor and Israel were at the opposite ends of the universal spectrum of the need to hate and the need for love, which extremes were interchangeable. One group can only truly hate another when it falsely loves itself. The Pamyat phenomenon, one that increases in all groups in times of economic hardship and political uncertainty, was a classic illustration of the tendency to blame another as one refuses to accept blame for oneself.

The manifestations of this universal populist *popaganda* whether it be in Jean Marie Le Pen's mightier than the sword National Front in France, in the Hitlerites National Socialism in Germany, in Political *Dukeplicity* in Louisiana, in God Gave Your Land to Me West Bank Settlers, or in Vasilyev's National Patriotic Front in Russia, are often metaphysically contradictory. Invariably, as evidenced by the banners and slogans in the Pamyat headquarters, the greatest good is used to justify the greatest evil and the highest love is used as a pretext for the basest hate. The reasons for this are explained at length in the novel, Crumbling Walls, by Vladimir's old friend, Dr. Ned Scott. Suffice it to conclude that its evil potential exists in all of us, and it can only be overcome by our metaphysical understanding of the metastasis of universal spiritual choice into self serving religious *chosenness* and ethnocentric *chosinness*. That metaphysical encounter within ourselves can lead to a universal spiritual realization that the only counter to ultimate evil is the ultimate good of one metaphysical good and one God for all versus one's God or good against all others.

Not only were lists being prepared about Jews in the Soviet Union, but they were also being prepared in the United States. Vladimir recalled a recent publication from private sources shown to him by Dr. Ned Scott, documenting the ethnic background of hidden Jews in the American establishment.

In one peculiar case, the name of the chairman of a recently merged communications conglomerate infused with Japanese capital was withheld from the Who's Who of Hidden Jews in the United States until conflicting reports about his ethnicity could be resolved. The files contained extensive personal along with professional information, as they had about the late and bogusly great Robert Maxwell. Maxwell, bogus to the literal extent of stealing his great Scots name, gave birth in his mysteriously untimely death to the timely economic principle of *Maxwellianism*. This *Maxwellian* economic principle personified the worst economic tendencies of *lousey* - faire capitalism, in its being defined as the Maximization of How Well I Am at the Expense of Others. These files contained personal information as to another caricature of the *Maxwellian* principle in the person of another media chairman in question, who attended both an Episcopal Church in New York and a Jewish Temple on Long Island. His name was Steve, and he was a bogusly ecumenical Steve for different religious occasions in signing his name differently in each house of worship.

It was reported that this person had attained a bonus of 75 million dollars in addition to his 3.3 million dollar income as a result of the merger which resulted in approximately 600 people losing their jobs. He made his personal bonus from the amount saved by eliminating 600 individual livelihoods. Apparently the group in question, itself hidden in their own Who's Not Who secret list of very unpopular and very violent populist groups, was concerned that they might have mistaken a reputable Wasp businessman for a disreputable Jew. It was a matter of concern to this group that they more thoroughly investigate his ethnicity, which fact, alone, would determine his degree of business ethics.

This danger of *groupism* is in no way limited to the Nazis or Pamyat or the KKK or to any one country or people. What is significant, however, is the difference between those groups who display the Christian Cross in flames of burning hate, and those that include Christians along with those others to be crucified. The Russian Pamyat and the American KKK present themselves in the cloak of Christianity whereas the Nazis, real Nazis, do not. The cold logic of the German *groupist* mind set determined in its initial formative stages that if Judaism were to be destroyed, Christianity would have to be eventually destroyed as well. For them, the Jews and the Christians were two birds of a slightly different feather who must be destroyed together.

Apparently similar movements in Russia and America never arrived at such a conclusion because they still wanted to consider themselves as defenders, somehow, of God himself. Those in Germany were not necessarily more fanatic, only more logical in their philosophy and more thorough in acting out the implications of that same hate. The German *groupists* knew that Christianity would eventually oppose them, whereas those in Russia and America actually thought that they were acting in the cause of Christianity. Thinking of Igor, he hoped he'd develop enough logic to realize that although hate may be as logical as it is destructive, hate in the name of Jesus is the ultimate illogic and moral contradiction. As long as there remained a connection, no matter how tenuous, to Jesus Christ, individual members of Pamyat like Igor might still be able to heal themselves by seeing the contradiction in themselves and turning away from their hate. If like the Nazis, however, he replaced a love of a perfect God with a love of his perfect self as part of his perfect group, there'd be no limit to his perfection of evil.

He'd taken most of the night talking to these tankers, each of whom chose to stay; and, now, he wondered who would choose to be the 36th unknown righteous man whose choice would help to make their choices a choice for others. As the morning sun started to rise, he could see that a brave new world rather than a grave new world could only develop to the extent that one heals what's inside as one repents on the outside. With the first rays of light, he saw Katharina walking over to him from her station on the barricades... seeing in her the light of his life.

"Ned was here earlier and told me to tell you he thinks he knows the 36th man."

"Did he say anything else?"

"No, only that he'd return as soon as he's sure."

"Katharina, I have an important question for you to answer right now," he looked at her, no longer afraid of what one fears most in oneself - one's own final choice.

"Will you marry me?"

"Only if you want me forever."

"Yes, I want you forever," he kissed her as he answered, in choosing love as a final choice.

CHAPTER NINETEEN

Irina, His Daughter, in Learning that Freedom Can Lead to Safety But Safety Can Never Lead to Freedom

As he held her, he felt a tap on his shoulder and turned to see his daughter, Irina, whom he was afraid he'd lost with Raisa.

"Father, as you probably guess, mother sent me here to bring you back, but I'm not here to do that, rather, I'm here to ask you as my father what I should do."

Irina Lubyanka was not only a physical creation of her parents but an ideological one as well, reflecting the very best of a very bad system. She was completing a Ph.D in the social sciences at Moscow State University and preparing to become an educator like her mother. Like her mother and unlike her father, she believed in the Gorbachev programs of glasnost and perestroika within the confines of the communist system that had been her ideological and personal sustenance.

"It took me over an hour to find you upon arriving here since all the soldiers were calling themselves Vladimir after you."

"I came with these men as a free man, Irina, rather than as their commanding officer, so that they could freely command themselves to come with me."

"I don't know what to do or think. I understand what you're fighting against, father, but I can't fight against the system I'm a part of," Irina responded, in looking and sounding more like daddy's little girl than the young women and university student she was.

"Vladimir, I'll see you after I organize some of the new young people arriving at the barricades," Katharina spoke, as she turned away without kissing him in respect to Irina, leaving her future husband, if they lived that long, alone, to speak with his only child and daughter.

"Irina, my dear, one has to know what to fight against before you can choose what to fight for. Your mother has chosen to stay with the old system, and I've chosen to fight against it as a way to begin a new fight for a new freedom in a new world for all of us. I'm not asking you, as my daughter, to fight my fight. But you, in return, can't ask me, as your father, to return to your mother, for that's her choice for me but not my choice for myself."

"No father, I can't and I won't, but I can ask you to help me decide what I should do."

"You have to choose for yourself, Irina."

"Our Marxist Leninist system has its faults, but so does the capitalist system of American Market Leninism. It's difficult for me as your daughter to make a choice between mother's Soviet Marxist Leninism and the American Market Leninism that I see as its replacement if these demonstrators at the barricades prevail."

"My dear, all of us, your mother, you and I were part of a system that mapped out everything so we always knew where we were going and how to get there without ever having to choose where we wanted to be. It wasn't a bad system in our case, but it was a system that did everything, as you just stated, to us rather than for us."

"So, dad, now that you've chosen for yourself, you're telling me that I have to choose for myself."

"Yes, my darling, if you want to be free, you have no other choice but to choose for yourself."

"This freedom that you're fighting for seems to be very simple, free and easy if you describe it as freedom from something, but much more complex if you try to define it as freedom to something."

"I'm not claiming that freedom of choice or freedom, itself, is simple or safe or easy... just the contrary. The price of freedom, Irina, is never free, and while freedom can lead to safety, safety can never lead to freedom."

Father, what does freedom mean if a person doesn't know where one's going or how to get there?"

"Irina, my dear, freedom means what you mean to make it. While there's an absolute freedom from everything and everyone, there's no absolute freedom to anything or anyone except oneself."

"And how, then, can you be free to yourself?"

Thinking of Katharina, he responded, "You can be free to heal yourself by being free enough to love another person in making a final free choice for that person in the same way you make a free choice of final love for yourself."

"Vladimir!" Katharina shouted fearfully, in interrupting them as she dragged a protesting seven year old boy with her, "this boy keeps telling me his name is Vladimir, like you, and he refuses to go home where he belongs to his mother."

"What's your name young man?" he sternly addressed the little boy, whose scruffy black hair covered a face even more blackened by the dirt from climbing on the barricades.

"Vladimir, like you sir."

"Well, Vladimir, do you know who I am?"

"Yes, sir, you're the real Vladimir."

"I am that and I know that you, too, can grow up to be a real Vladimir like me someday, for I'm very proud of you," as he spoke the young boy's face beamed in delight through all the dust and dirt.

"Do you know what it means to be a real Vladimir?"

"Yes, sir, . . . it means bringing tanks like yours to fight."

"That may be true for an old Vladimir like me, but for a young Vladimir like you it means something else."

"Yes, sir," the boy looked up at him intently, as Irina went over to hold him as Katharina handed the boy over to her.

"It means that you have to choose to do what's right for your mother who's very worried because she doesn't know where you are now. A real Vladimir has to protect his worried mother by going home to her so he can grow up to fight another day and, hopefully, in another way."

"I will sir."

"Father, I'll take him home," Irina spoke, as she lifted up the boy, "that's my choice."

"Irina, my dear daughter, you've just given your own answer to your own question as to how to be free to yourself. Your answer is your choice to teach children that they can always choose and never have to be chosen."

Vladimir watched Irina take the child away confident that his daughter would be free where his wife had failed. He was confident in the knowledge that no one can be chosen by advantage, or *chosin* by disadvantage, as long as all children know that they must chose such that no one can be considered chosen or *chosin*.

CHAPTER TWENTY

The Unknown Righteous Man

"I've found the 36th unknown righteous man," the unmistakable voice of Ned Scott announced, as he returned to the barricades through the same passage that Irina had just left with the little boy.

"Praise the Lord! he must be a Pentecostal to be able to descend down upon us at our moment of need," Vladimir joyfully replied.

"Well, although it's true he's a man of some power and fire, it's far more earthly firepower than any fire or power of the Holy Spirit."

"What do you mean Ned?"

"He's the commander of the Alpha Group, who in hearing about a certain unknown Vladimir and his tanks refused repeated direct orders to attack."

They stood together knowing that whatever might happen next, what'd already happened had given everyone more light to see the vision of their freedom to choose.

"For a military man just like yourself, Vladimir, you know how much courage it takes to say no to such an order."

"You're right, Ned, and it takes new insight," he responded, seeing in unknown others the literal fulfillment of his mother's vision.

"That's not all the good news I have for you, there's much more."

How ironic, he reflected, how the threat of impending death can be transformed by the choice of a vision into the vision of a choice for oneself, others, one's country and, yes, for the world.

"Patriarch Aleksy II as the head of the Russian Orthodox Church has spoken out against the coup as the first Patriarch ever to speak out in this regard. The KGB's Vitebskaya Division has stopped in their tracks just a few miles from here. General Pavel Grachev, Chief of Airborne troops, has also refused an order to attack the Russian Parliament. He was joined by the Aviation Minister, Air Force Commander General Gennadi Shaposhnikov, who in response to an order its bomb the White House replied that if he were to bomb anything, it would be the Kremlin."

"Last and best news of all, General Alexander Lebed of the Tula Division has sent more tanks and APCs to surround the Russia Parliament with a protective shield of armor. Their guns, which will be empty for now, will face out from the White House in sending your message to the world."

While it would take one more night until Boris Yeltsin announced the next day on Wednesday, August 21, 1991, that the coupspiracy was over, Vladimir knew it had already been beaten by vision…his mother's vision. Her vision became his own, then Ned's, and, now, the growing vision of countless others on both sides of the barricades. Katharina, too, had her vision first, long before he could see, as she could, the reality of freedom and love.

Tragically for a few soldiers and civilians, three men died that Tuesday night when the crowds mistook a withdrawing armored column as moving to attack the White House. Tensions were high and many ordinary Muscovites ran up to the tanks and plastered them with slogans stating, "USSR - Shame." A retired Russian admiral who was walking by, threw his overcoat over the tank slit to obstruct its vision, and one of the soldiers panicked in shooting a young man who'd climbed on top of the tank. Two other men were crushed to death under an overpass as a tank driver tried to escape the crowds and threw his tank into the wrong gear, in not seeing the men between the tank and the underpass wall.

Both those who killed by mistake and killed in error fought each other in confusion. Let the memories of these three brave young men, who died fighting the coup, remain memorialized as a lesson to all of us how easy death can occur when ideas about freedom remain confused.

Also, let us realize that the crimes of the coup did not begin nor end in the three days during which the vision of a Mother Russia of freedom was entombed only to prophetically rise on the third day… as Vera Lubyanka saw it would.

Dr. Ned Scott, American professor, criminologist, peacebroker, and most of all, friend of freedom, left his friend Vladimir with a new task and a new fight for the Russian way back and ahead to freedom. Russia would be free to open herself to freedom in direct proportion to the extent that she would face her past. She would have to heal herself on the inside in order to face a future of freedom with all those outside.

CHAPTER TWENTY-ONE

Soviet Banksters

Four days after the abortive coup, one Nicolai Kruchina was thrown from the window of his seventh floor apartment by "unknown assailants", and on the same day his superior, Oleg Shenin, was quickly whisked away in an official limousine. Shenin, a Politburo number and financial controller for the Communist Party, was personally in charge of huge currency and gold transfers in the hundreds of billions of dollars. Reliable criminological sources indicate that he was able to internationally launder funds for Communist party leaders who might be driven into exile. Kruchina, who'd been Soviet Administrator of the Central Business Directorate in Moscow, handled not only the funds of the Soviet government, but the secret accounts of the Communist Party as well.

The question remains as to how the immense Soviet gold reserves were lost and the answer lies in discovering how they were laundered.

Grigory Yavlinsky, Chief of the Soviet Delegation to the annual conference of the International Monetary Fund and the World Bank in Bangkok, Thailand, announced that Soviet gold reserves had dwindled to 240 tons. Just 6 years before, Soviet reserves had been reported to total more than 2,600 tons. Finally in November of 1991, Alexander Orlov, head of the Soviet parliament's audit commission announced that "our specialists have analyzed the situation with gold and arrived at the conclusion that the State Bank of the Soviet Union is bankrupt."

This disappearance of Soviet holdings of bullion makes any Mafia conspiracy look like a small time amateur operation in comparison to the coupspiracy. The next fight for Vladimir and his righteous men would be that of getting the money back, a far more difficult one than fighting the coup. Neither the Kremlin's lousey - failed communism nor the gremlins of the shared-monopoly game of lousey-failing capitalism would be of any assistance. In chasing down the Chase Bank trail of the coupspiracy, Vladimir, with a rare righteous associate in ass kicking Kissinkick's Associates, would discover that many former international socialists would hide out in the Pamyat House for neo-national socialists as Pamrats. They were not the first Communists to go to bed with Nazis, just as, conversely, in the former East German undemocratic Democratic Republic, former Nazis found a house of refuge in neo-Communism.

Like Adolph Hitler before him, Boris Pugo committed suicide along with others such as General Sergei Akhromeyev rather than chose to live for the new vision of a rising freedom. Raisa had chosen them as representatives of system she loved over the man she'd loved and committed her own emotional suicide in the process. He didn't care to see her again, but he did care that she would eventually see for herself.

The military contingents were looking for ways to withdraw throughout the early and mid-morning hours until the tension abated when Boris Yeltsin announced at exactly 2:15 p.m. on Wednesday, August 21, 1919, that the coup was over.

As crowds surged in front of the White House, Katharina and Vladimir embraced in their final choice to be free for and in each other. A young student who'd manned the barricades with her since Monday realized that he didn't even know her name, and he ran up to her as she started to walk away with Vladimir.

"Excuse me, but I never had time to ask who you were when you were helping us," a tall blond young man around twenty years of age spoke up.

"Can you tell me who you are and what you plan to do in the future?" he inquired.

"Young man, I can answer both your questions," she responded by hugging Vladimir even closer, "by telling you that I'm the future Mrs. Vladimir . . . that's all you and I need to know."

CHAPTER TWENTY-TWO

No New World Order But a Personal Order For a New World

As Vladimir and the future Mrs. Vladimir left the barricades and disappeared into the crowds, he no longer felt any barricade inside to his love for her and the reality of his own freedom. He was free to love knowing that the price of love or freedom is never free and knowing that the truth of freedom may hurt but cannot destroy if one doesn't lie to oneself. It might be true that he sinned, but it's also true that it's better to love in sin than to sin in love. He would heal himself by love but never from love, and never away from her love.

Freedom can lead to safety but safety can never lead to freedom. Vladimir and Katharina might never be safe again but they'd be free. He hoped for the safety of peace, but he would not forget that a false peace at the price of real freedom is a false freedom at the price of real peace. The absolutely right answer to the absolutely right question about love and freedom he saw with in and through her, is that freedom in love is neither love nor freedom, but freedom to love is both love and freedom. No coup can last if both are inside, if not, no man nor woman can last.

Ned was right about the absolute – it's always there but never fixed in any time, place, land, people, church, creed or book. The absolute of freedom is never stationery, never another's statue of liberty, but ever one's own stature of liberty wherein each individual determines his own personal station in life by internalizing the absolute of love, the ultimate of God, outside, with the freedom to love, inside. While there is an absolute freedom from everything and everyone, there is no absolute freedom to anything or anyone, except oneself; and while love solves nothing, it heals everything.

In order not to be absolutized by the world's order in doing wrong in the name of right - man's religious and secular final solutions - one must do right by oneself and others by taking one's freedom without taking others. The ultimate freedom from centering God on ourselves is to enter ourselves and our God on others freedom.

In contrast to man's history - his story and her story of evil as the inversion of live - a history of the world's order, the future order for the world (he could now see his mother's vision) would not be an impersonal new world order, but something far better, a personal order for a new world.

Vladimir showed us that the best personal order is not laying down one's life for another but, rather, picking it up for others. Any world order by its oxymoronic definition is an insanity that can never be saved by sanity, but only by a higher insanity. The final solution for our world and for its old and new order is the insanity of love without which life in any world is insane.

As Ned watched them walk away together into the crowds he could see their choice for each other as the way for others choice for themselves. No person could be considered chosin if no people considered themselves chosen. Either our world will coupspire against itself with an old Amen to a So Be It to being chosen, or free itself with a new Amen to a Be It So of having chosen.

"Amen," Ned said to himself, to them, to the crowds and to the future hope of a resurrected Mother Russia as a mother of freedom for the world.

APPENDIX

QUOTES FROM THE PHYSICAL TO THE METAPHYSICAL

1 Absolutes

a. The proposition that there is no absolute is, in itself, an absolute proposition.

b. The absolute was ever present but never fixed.

c. A new and final moment of truth occurs when there's a new moment in life and final moment beyond life for a final moment of truth about life.

2 Anti-Semitism

a. Jesus was a Jew who started Judeo-Christianity, in response to which Jews who liked Jesus were persecuted by Jews and Gentiles alike. Thereafter, Gentile Christians saw Jews as Christ killers, and Christ as a killer, in killing Jews in the name of their Jewish Messiah. Finally, the post-Christian Final Solution of the Holocaust held Jews to be guilty for not only Judaism and Communism, but for the pre-Christian original sin of Jewish originated Christianity.

3 Bad Taste

a. The extent to which bad taste becomes good business in America is astonishing.

4 Boris the Yellsin

a. Boris the Yellsin: Boris Yeltsin could Yell Sin better than any prophet at any freedom revival anywhere, in making a new name for himself as Boris theYellsin. He yelled sin for all to hear, in baring the sins of Communism, in calling all to repent with a penitential refrain of freedom for all.

5 Buddhist Buddies

a. Buddhist Buddies and Seoul-Soul Brothers spoken by a Kazakhstan man to Vladimir: I hoped that maybe a Korean

Buddhist from Seoul could help us become Buddies- Muslim, Christian, Jewish- to be Soul brothers together. I would have included Marxists, but, unlike the Marx Brothers, they're got no soul and they're not very funny.

6 Choice and Chosenness

a. Teach children that they can always choose and never have to be chosen.

b. No one can own the chosenness of God's love, but everyone can choose it as their own.

7 Death

a. Everyone has to choose how to face death in order to live.

8 Evil

a. Evil is literally defined as the inverted spelling of Live…in evil inverting life.

b. When one limits the love of a perfect God to one's perfect self in one's perfect group, one removes all limits to perfect evil.

9 Faith, God and Belief

a. There are no unbelievers anywhere, for everyone believes in something they can't prove.

b. Faith, like love, goes beyond rational choice to irrational need culminating in supernatural good.

c. An omniscient God would certainly know enough to stock heaven with plenty of Russian vodka if nothing else.

d. The distinction between an old time religion and an all time religion is that the former reacts with an old faith in a limited future, whereas the latter activates all that's best in the present with a new faith in an unlimited future.

e. Christianity is false on the outside if Jesus isn't truly inside, for without Jesus life is spiritually insane.

f. Either there's one God for all or one's God against all others.

g. Any one can be perfected by God but no one can be perfect.

10 Freedom

a. Freedom can only be won by fighting for one's own stature of liberty rather than someone else's statue of liberty.

b. While freedom can lead to safety, safety can never lead to freedom.

c. The right question to the wrong answer of freedom is how to take one's freedom without taking others freedom away.

d. The freedom to be unfree in one freedom, to conform to one free prefixed free process, is not freedom.

e. Freedom comes from the soul, and with one's soul rationalization is irrational, and rationing is a short fall ratio that can never go far enough for one can never ration one's soul.

f. The ultimate freedom from centering God on ourselves is to enter ourselves and our God on others freedom.

11 Freedom and Choice

a. There's no guarantee that a free choice is a right choice, only that freedom begins with choice.

b. Freedom guarantees choice, but choice does not guarantee freedom.

12 Hate

a. One group can truly hate another only when it falsely loves itself.

b. Although hate may be as logical as it is destructive, hate in the name of Jesus is the ultimate illogic and the most destructive religious contradiction.

13 Katharina

a. Katherina (Vladimir's lover): You might describe me as the soon to be divorced missing Mrs. who doesn't miss being a Mrs.

b. Katherina toVladimir: You may be an unknown Vladimir to the world, but to me you're the Vladimir I know who has made my world.

14 Kissinkick ASSsociates

a. The leading asses of Kissinkick Associates (who got their name Kissinkick in commemoration of a former Secretary of State, Henry Kissinger, who perfected the real ass politics of kissing big ass and kicking little ass) were Brent Socrafty and Lawrence Eataburger the third. It was discovered that so skinny Socrafty never ate burgers while Eataburger ate excessive third helpings. The CIA had designated Eataburger as their biggest Central Intelligent Ass, with his intelligence centered in his ass. Due to the fact that Eataburger was such a smart ass, the CIA ordered extra burgers from Burger King for all CIA special ass assets in wanting to create more smart asses.

15 Love

a. Freedom in love is not the same as freedom to love.

b. Better than laying down one's life for another, pick it up to love another.

c. Better to love in sin than sin in love.

d. What one expects in love is not love.

e. How easy it is to be controlled by love, but how difficult it is to control love.

f. One can be emptied of love but only filled by it.

g. How quickly one runs in love and stumbles to love.

h. Love is never sane, but always wonderfully insane, in the insanity of love without which life is insane.

16 Love and Freedom

a. What an unfortunate anomaly between the sexes that the male is free to be aggressive and equal with equal contradiction, whereas only the female is free to be aggressively equal without contradiction.

b. While love creates freedom, lovingness creates control in the name of love and the place of freedom.

17 Marxism

a. One always knew what was absolutely right in Marxism, even when you knew you were required to do what was absolutely wrong.

b. Vladimir knew from experience that Marxism, by fixating morality on its process, by moralizing any means to its end, ended as it began in amorality.

c. The problem with Vladimir's wife, her family and their Marxism was that while they tried to correct what was wrong, they could never see what was right: the more good they did to others, the more bad those others felt.

d. Among all peoples there is a universal belief in belief, most of all among unbelievers, who, like the Marxists, in disavowing the belief of other creeds, create their own belief in the collective creed of all good residing in themselves.

e. Marx was right about religion being used as the opiate of the people, but he left out the fact that his quasi-religious Manifesto was the worst drug of all.

18 Maxwelliamism

a. Maxwelliamism: The late and bogusly great Robert Maxwell, bogus to the literal extent of stealing his great Scots name, gave birth in his untimely death to the deadly economic principle of Maxwelliamism. This Maxwelliam economic principle personified the worst economic tendencies of lousez-faire capitalism in its being defined as the Maximization of How Well I Am at the expense of others.

19 Men and Women

a. Women don't leave bad men, they leave good men.

b. They were equal in the best way a man and a woman could be equal…in love.

c. The worst problem for the best wife is a better husband.

d. Whereas women prefer strength over goodness in a man, men prefer goodness over strength in a woman.

e. The worst problem for a perfect woman is a more perfect husband, such that the best woman can endure anything except a better husband.

20 Metaphysical

a. Metaphysical: One's metaphysical encounter within oneself can lead to an universal spiritual realization that the only counter to ultimate evil is the ultimate good of one metaphysical good or God for all versus one's God or good against all others.

21 Mother Russia

a. Russia died in 1917, but Mother Mary came to me with a vision that Mother Russia would rise once again.

b. The vision of his mother was the Icon of Mother Russia, and like her the Icon was old and near dead, but still alive.

22 Peace

a. The ideology of the person rather than of the people is the way to peace.

b. A false peace at the price of real freedom is a false freedom at the price of real peace.

23 Prayer

a. A real prayer sees beyond the past and a present determined by the past to a present determination for the future.

b. The old Amen is an unfree So Be It to being chosen, whereas the new Amen is a free Be It So to having chosen.

24 Religion

a. Fundamentalism in any religion destroys the fundamentals of human respect for others.

b. God's Promised Land is any land with the promise of God's freedom.

25 Right and Wrong

a. Why do those who talk so much about what's right, seem to be the same ones who do so much that's wrong?

b. The answer to the dilemma past, present and future of why so much wrong is proclaimed in the name of right, of who so much evil is done in the name of good, of why so many final solutions of death are imposed by those with new manifestos of life is that their absolutely right answers proceed from absolutely wrong questions.

26 Safe Sex

a. One can have safe sex but not safe love.

27 Sex in Russia and America

a. Whereas Americans laugh at love and try to be serious about sex, Russians take love seriously and laugh about sex.

28 Small Nations

a. Better to live in a small nation in a big world of freedom than live in a small world of big nations with little freedom.

b. Latvia: Our capital Riga was an example to the world as to how Soviet Rigamortis killed individual initiative.

29 Ukraine and Chicken Kiev

a. A Ukrainan speaking to Vladimir: I intend to take our stand here at these barricades as a stand for dismantling barricades between people.

b. Same Ukranian speaking to Vladimir: President George H. Bush visited the Ukraine and delivered his Chicken Kiev speech in warning us Ukes, in Bush League fashion, about the dangers of our own need for national freedom.

30 Vision

a. How ironic, Vladimir reflected, how the threat of impending death can be transformed by the choice of a vision into the vision of a choice for oneself, others, one's country and, yes, for the world.

31 Vladimir

a. Vladimir: At Tiananmen, the world watched one unknown man stand against a tank. Now, the world watched one unknown man, who said Just Call Me Vladimir, take his stand in his tank, in standing against the full military forces of the Soviet Union, in standing in union with the people.

b. Vladimir: Some unknown tank commander in positioning his tank to defend rather than attack freedom had changed the moral odds that changed the military odds that changed the world. The man who changed everything in the world remained unknown to the world, in referring to himself as Just Call Me Vladimir.

c. Vladimir: When others see my personal order for myself, they'll see themselves differently. They'll fight not at my order or others orders, or for an old or new world order, but they'll fight because of my order as their order for themselves.

d. Vladimir: I don't want to continue to be your Lt. Colonel Tank Commander, instead, Just Call Me Vladimir, a man who can order himself for others to follow in freedom, and to follow to freedom.

e. Vladimir: Look to your ancient Icon of Mother Russia as your modern "Ican" to Russian freedom.

f. Vladimir: Together, we will all be unknown Vladimirs, unknown righteous men who freely choose more than a new world order in choosing our personal order for a new world of freedom.

32 Vladimir speaking to Muslims, Lutherans, Catholics and Jews

Vladimir speaking to his tank commanders of differing religions about religion:

a. To Muslims: No soul, the Koran states, can die except by Allah's leave and at a time appointed. The appointed time is now my brothers, for now is the point in time for you to choose in your own way, in your own decision for life and death, what Allah asks of you.

152

b. To Lutherans: Like Luther, who fought personal demons and transformed the demons of his time, we have to fight our demons and transform those who deny political democracy with their Communist demonocracy.

c. To Catholics: You believe in and pray to saints who showed what God was so that others might see what they might be. Today is your Holy Day of Obligation, a day obligated by your choice to be holy in taking freedom from a holistic concept to a wholly Real Presence.

d. To Jews: The Talmud states that to show mercy to the cruel is to show cruelty to the innocent. The innocents are waiting at the barricades and not to act, now, in their defense is to condone the cruelty of their slaughter.

e. A Jewish prophecy for saving the world: That 36th righteous man would be needed to save all of them and, accordingly, save the world in the process. That was what the Jewish prophecy said, and even though he wasn't a Jewish believer…he believed the Jewish prophecy.

33 World Order vs. New World

a. The future order for the world would not be an impersonal new world order, but something far better, a personal order for a new world.

NEW WORDS, CONCEPTS, AND DEFINITIONS

APPARAT Apparat refers to the rat like qualities of Soviet Officialdumb as evidenced by the front man for the Vosmyorka, The Gang of Eight, Gennadi "SS" Yanayev, with "SS" standing for sap and sob.

CANVINCED Canvinced and Canvincement refer to one's process of going beyond being convinced, in agreeing with a proposition, to one of knowing one can personally achieve or attain it.

CHOSENNESS vs. CHOSINNESS Chosenness is described as the universal spiritual choice of one God for all in opposition to Chosinness, described as the self serving sinful choice of one's God against all others.

CHOSIN Chosin refers to the sin of presuming to be what God never assumed to be.

CHOSINNESS Chosinness is defined as the sinful choice of choosing one God as one's God, only

DEMONOCRACY Demonocracy refers to the demonic imposition of communism upon democracy.

EATABURGER Eataburger is an insider reference at burger joints to Lawrence Eataburger the 3rd, a fat ass of Kissinkick Associates, who would always eat 3rd helpings of burgers.

FRAUDIAN Fraudian refers to the fraud of Freudian "Odd Studying the Id" pseudo-psychology.

GROUPISM Groupism refers to the process of defining one's self through one's group.

HARMACEUTICAL Harmaceutical refers to the harmful effects of the Pharmaceutical Industry in exploiting illness for profit.

ICON as ICAN Ican refers to the choice of the Russian Icon as a personal Ican to Russian freedom.

JESUSANITY Jesusanity refers to Jesus as the way to sanity.

JUSTUS Justus is defined as justice for one's group only.

KISSINKICK Kissinkick refers to a former Secretary of State who earned his name by kissing fat ass and kicking little ass.

LOUSEY- FAIRE Lousey-faire refers to what's lousey with laissez-faire capitalism.

MARXIST and MARKET LENINISM Marxist Leninism refers to the failed political totalitarianism of Soviet Communism and Market Leninism refers to the failing economic totalitarianism of so called Free Trade Capitalism.

MAXWELLIAM Maxwelliam is defined as maximizing how well I am by minimizing others.

MOSCOUP Moscoup refers to the attempt to reverse the reforms of Mikhail Gorbachev that was initiated by a Communist coup that began at 7:00 am. August 19, 2001, and ended at 5:00 pm. August 21, 2001.

OFFICIALDUMB Officialdumb refers to the human product of officialism wherein the dumbest of the officious become officials.

PAMRAT Pamrat refers to a political Soviet rat who rats out on international socialism and rats in on neo-national socialism in becoming a rat for all political seasons.

PARISTOCITIC NOABILITY The parasitic aristocracy of the noability of inherited wealth with no ability other than living off the ability of others.

PAVLOVIAN Pavlovian refers to the tendency of Valentine Pavlov, as former Soviet Minister, to drool and pig out under pressure.

PHARISTOCITIC Pharistocitic is defined as self righteousness in religious and secular aristocracies.

POPAGANDA Popaganda refers to the popular projection of propaganda by means of pop media.

RIGAMORTIS Rigamortis refers to the deadly stiffening of the body politic as a result of the Soviet occupation of Riga, Latvia.

SOCRAFTY Socrafty refers to Brent Socrafty, a little ass at Kissinkick Associates, who was known to be so crafty.

THOROUGHRED Thoroughred describes a thoroughbred Red, a purebred Communist.

TRUTH BELIEVER vs. TRUE BELIEVER The truth believer is described as one who goes beyond all true believers to one who believes in one truth for all.

VILENIUS Vilenius refers to the vile legacy of the Soviet occupation of Vilnius, Lithuania.

YELLSIN Yellsin refers to Boris "The Yellsin" Yeltsin, who yelled sin about all the sins of the Communists with a refrain of freedom for all.

END NOTE ON CHAPTER 17

i   The scientific data and all descriptive information as to people, places and events from pages 99-106 were obtained from the First International Baltic Forum of NGOs, Nov. 1990 and from the International Baltic Ecological Forum of NGOs. May 1991.